Red High Heels
in Heaven

Red High Heels in Heaven

Deanna Hill

authorHOUSE®

AuthorHouse™
1663 Liberty Drive
Bloomington, IN 47403
www.authorhouse.com
Phone: 1-800-839-8640

First published by AuthorHouse   09/21/2011

ISBN: 978-1-4634-0708-7 (sc)
ISBN: 978-1-4634-0707-0 (hc)
ISBN: 978-1-4634-0706-3 (ebk)

Library of Congress Control Number: 2011907370

Printed in the United States of America

Any people depicted in stock imagery provided by Thinkstock are models, and such images are being used for illustrative purposes only.
Certain stock imagery © Thinkstock.

This book is printed on acid-free paper.

Because of the dynamic nature of the Internet, any web addresses or links contained in this book may have changed since publication and may no longer be valid. The views expressed in this work are solely those of the author and do not necessarily reflect the views of the publisher, and the publisher hereby disclaims any responsibility for them.

CONTENTS

Part One 1

  Chapter One 1

  Chapter Two 5

  Chapter Three 8

  Chapter Four 13

  Chapter Five 16

  Chapter Six 20

Part Two 25

Part Three 63

Part Four 107

Part Five 113

ACKNOWLEDGEMENTS

Special thanks to . . .

The longest "prayer chain" in the world. Thank you for your cards, letters, love, encouragement and most of all prayers. God heard and He honored those prayers. You are a very large and important part of the miracle that I am.

Orthopedist Dr. Jerrold Lancourt, surgical assistant Dick McLaughlin, orthopedist Dr. Michael Trueblood, physical therapist, nurses, nurse aids and care givers in both hospitals, thank you for your excellent care. You too are a very important part of the miracle that I am.

FORWARD

Thank you Deanna for providing this beautiful window to your heart and soul. Shining light not only on the tragedy that life has presented to you, but insight as to how the sustaining and overcoming grace of God can lift you above and beyond adversity.

Even Jesus had to make a decision at his worst moment to accept or reject the plan of His Father no matter what. Truly you have been made more like Him. For with each and every trial of life, a little more, you have learned to trust.

All who read your amazing story will in some way read theirs as well, and maybe, just maybe learn to trust in Him.
—Ronny Hinson

DEDICATION

To Helen Jo. I list you first in this dedication for in reality, we wrote the book together. Without your detailed journal of the accident in the early part of my hospitalization and recovery, I would not have had all of the information I needed. Thank you for that and for "standing in the gap" for me when I could not. Without your spunk to speak up and refuse to accept the medical guidelines prescribed for my treatment, I would not be walking today. You have been through it all with me and you have my sincere thanks and undying gratitude. You're the best sister in the world and my best "girl friend". I love you.

To my husband, Kenny. Your love and assurance from the very beginning of my recovery until the present, have helped me deal with my pain, limitations and scars. When we began our married life in January of 1960 we enjoyed many years of joy and laughter. It was only after January 25, 1986 that we encountered many tears and sorrows. I could not have made it without your love, strength and assurance. We have laughed together and cried together. You are my best friend and I pray we will have many more wonderful, happy and healthy years together. I love you "old guy".

To Mark and Geinger, my "kids". You were there for me too. Mark, you were always a delightfully funny and talented little kid. You have given me so much joy, from that funny little kid to the wonderful man you have become. I could not be more proud of you. When you brought Geinger into our lives and our family, our joy was doubled. Geinger, you are the best daughter-in-law anybody ever had. Your loving and sweet spirit is as beautiful as you are. And when Jacob Gregory and Ethan Kent came along they brought a new kind of love and joy into my life. You boys continue to amaze and delight me. What fun it is being your Daw Daw.

Mark, Geinger, Jake and "E", I love the four of you more than you will ever know.

To Mom and Daddy, thanks for your love, encouragement and prayers throughout the years. Thanks for raising me in a Christian home. That solid spiritual foundation helped prepare me for the trials to come later in my life and to be able to handle them. What a blessing you have been and continue to be.

To the memory of my son Kent, I miss your sense of humor, your wonderful smile, your talent and your sweet spirit. You are forever in my heart and mind.

PART ONE

Chapter One

It was very cold the night of January 24, 1986. Cold enough for the diesel fuel in the bus to gel and make it difficult to start. Finally a little before 9:00 PM the guys had it running and we all boarded and pulled out on schedule for concerts in Nebraska.

Though no one mentioned it at the time, some of the members of our family, as well as the band, had an uneasy feeling about the upcoming trip and thought perhaps we should cancel and reschedule for a later date with better weather conditions. However, being taught all of our lives to fulfill obligations if at all possible, no one voiced their concerns. We felt we had to go.

After the last minute scramble to board the bus and stow the food and our gear everyone began to settle in for the long trip. Kent was not feeling well from a sinus infection and was the first to crawl into his bunk. Greg and Brad were not far behind him. Steve had the first shift driving and Mark was riding in the buddy seat keeping him company.

Helen Jo and I were in our room in the back of the bus visiting. Even though we lived next door to each other, most of our quality time together was on the bus. While we talked Helen Jo gave herself a manicure and I sewed fasteners on a couple of stage dresses I had made that week. When I finished with them I too did my fingernails and even indulged myself in a pedicure, painting my toenails the same pearly pink color I had used on my fingernails.

As we settled into our bunks for the night, everything was quiet. The only noise was the hum of the engine directly behind our room and the road noises made by our tires and those of the other night travelers.

1

Hopefully we would be able to sleep well and get as many hours as possible before arriving in Hastings, Nebraska the next day.

At approximately 4:50 AM, the morning of January 25th, we had been traveling for almost 8 hours. We had made one stop for fuel in Cape Girardeau, MO, and a second stop near St. Louis to replace a fuse to the back interior lights. The roads had been clear and there had been very little traffic. We were making good time. Brad, who had taken Mark's place in the buddy seat in St. Louis, and Steve were getting tired. Steve pulled into a truck stop south of St. Joseph, MO and woke Greg and me to take their places. Ordinarily Helen Jo and I did not take a turn during the night sitting with the driver but since Kent was not feeling well we were giving him time to rest and get better before the upcoming concerts. After the brief stop we were back on I-29 by 5:00 AM. Greg told me he had slept well and was in good shape. He encouraged me to get as comfortable as possible in my seat and try to nap if I could. Everyone knew I never slept well, if at all, as long as the bus was moving. With my pillow and blanket, I got cozy, slumped down in the seat enough to prop my feet on the door hinge and rest.

Four miles outside of St. Joseph, MO our headlights reflected off of something in the road ahead. Assuming it was a barricade warning of roadwork Greg slowed down and began to ease into the left lane. I sat up straight in my seat as we both tried to figure out exactly what we were seeing. The next instant we realized it was not a barricade but an 18-wheel semi-trailer truck completely blocking both of our north bound lanes. Our headlights were reflecting off of a stainless steel tanker. There were no lit running lights on the side of the tanker, no visible headlights because the metal guardrail had wrapped around them on impact, no warning flares on the roadway and no one flagging traffic. No warning whatsoever of the imminent danger. Almost as one Greg and I said, "My God, we're gonna hit it!"

Greg swung a hard left on the steering wheel trying for the median and literally stood on the brakes, locking them up, but the 18-wheeler had plowed up chunks of mud as it crossed the median, throwing them onto the roadway. When our tires contacted the mud it was like being on ice and we had no traction. We hit the tanker dead center, bounced off and hit it again.

Things seemed to be happening in slow motion. The glass from the windshield looked like an ocean wave coming toward us as it shattered all the way across. I remember turning my head and throwing my arm across my eyes and the thought went through my mind, "This is what it's like to die . . . today I'll see Jesus." I was not afraid. Greg had also turned his head and put his arm over his eyes when he saw the glass shattering. One of those things one does instinctively and I'm sure it saved our eyes from damage as we were showered with the glass of the windshield. I was also hit with wood and metal from the dash in front of me as well as the metal door on the right, front side of the bus where I was sitting.

It was immediately evident that I was injured as I was calling for help and pleading for someone to get me out. I kept repeating over and over, "Oh, my legs. Oh, God they hurt so bad. Oh, my legs, I don't want them to be broken. Please somebody help me. I'm so cold." I was fully conscious and experiencing horrible pain like nothing I had ever felt before. I remember saying at one point that labor pains hadn't hurt as badly.

Part of the dash had been broken loose and pushed inward in front of Greg and the steering wheel was slightly bent to the left making very tight quarters for him. He was a little disoriented and confused from the impact, but I don't think he ever lost consciousness. He could not move out of his seat. My legs were pinned in tight and I could not move in any way. I kept pushing on the metal bar in front of me trying to move it off.

The other members of the band, Steve sleeping on the lounge sofa, Kent, Mark and Brad sleeping in their bunks in the mid section of the bus, and Helen Jo sleeping in our room in the very back of the bus, were awakened by three very loud and consecutive booms and jolts. The first impact had broken everything loose across the front and right, front side of the bus crushing it inward. Parts of the dash in front of Greg were jammed down on the accelerator, which had caused the bus to hit the truck the second time and kept the engine revving. It sounded like a jet plane just before take off. Much of the lounge section of the bus was also very damaged.

Kent, Mark and Brad had been tossed around in their bunks, which shook them up a bit, but they were uninjured. They crawled from their bunks and began trying to open the door between their quarters and the lounge area but it was jammed. As they finally got it open and scrambled through, they had to climb over debris in the lounge area to get to the front where Greg and I were sitting. Helen Jo jumped from her top bunk, also unharmed and fumbled in the dark to put her socks and shoes on before coming forward. Everyone was thinking at that time that we had probably run into a ditch.

3

Steve was uninjured though he had been thrown from the couch, across the aisle, to the other side of the bus. He was the first one to Greg and me, closely followed by Kent. While Steve was trying to help me, Kent was assessing the situation and firing questions, "Greg, are the flashers on?" Greg answered, "Yes." Kent again, "What's in that tank?" Someone answered, "It's an empty milk tanker." The answer had come from the driver of the truck who was standing in the median on the left side of the bus. Everyone breathed a sigh of relief to learn it was not full of something flammable or toxic. I'm sure it was a blessing too that it was empty and not loaded. Kent then sent Brad out to flag traffic so no one would hit us from behind.

I was still begging and pleading for them to get me out, telling them how badly my legs were hurting and that we could not see the truck because there were no running lights. Then I would pray that God would not let my legs be broken. I was actually thinking that if they were not broken we could still make the concerts in Nebraska.

Greg was nauseated and still a bit groggy but was trying to get out of his seat. Someone told him to try and slide his seat back and maybe he could get out that way. It worked and he was able to get up and walk back to the lounge area and sit down. I was relieved to see him walk because that meant his legs were not broken. He continued to complain about nausea as well as needing to get his contact lenses out. Helen Jo went after his bag with his contact supplies and eyeglasses. She also gave him a bowl in case he had to throw up. He was covered with glass.

Helen Jo ministered to him as well as me, keeping us talking and trying to keep us warm. She later said she knew there were three things she needed to do to prevent shock, but she could only remember two of them . . . keep the person warm and conscious. The third one she could not remember, was to elevate the feet. She got more blankets for us and continued to talk to both of us, telling us not to pass out on her. The pain was so terrible I was hoping I would. In fact, I remember praying, "Oh, God, please let me pass out." Helen Jo would have none of that, she said, "No you're not, keep talking to me, stay awake."

Steve and Kent were working trying to remove the debris off of me so they could get me out of the seat and back to the couch. However, they could not budge the metal or the wood. They would need something to pry the metal off me. Steve went out through the hole where the windshield had been to get a cheater bar from one of the bays under the bus. A cheater bar is a long metal bar used to pry lug nuts loose on the tires of big rigs. It was the best option they had to try to move the wood and especially the metal.

Chapter Two

I was born to Milton and Virginia Pecord on February 17, 1941 and raised in a little farming community in southern Illinois. Dad farmed and Mom was a housewife. Up to the age of 14, I was an only child. Then on January 28, 1955, when I was a freshman in High School, Mom presented me with a baby sister, Helen Jo. She was not quite 5 years old when my husband, Kenneth, and I married January 16, 1960 in the small country church I had attended all of my life. We began our married life in the Strategic Air Command of the U. S. Air Force, stationed at Forbes Air Force Base in Topeka, KS where we lived for 10 months. When his tour of duty was up we moved back to southern Illinois where we had both been born and raised, he in Desoto and me in Miller City, 60 miles apart.

Kenny and I had met when he was fifteen years old and I was ten when Jerry Smith, the son of a former pastor, who had relocated to DeSoto, brought Kenny and two or three other young men to meet my Dad who operated a goose hunting club. All of the guys loved to hunt, especially geese and ducks. Kenny and a couple of others became guides for Daddy during the fall hunting season when the Canadian geese migrated to our area.

Until I was seventeen years old Kenny treated me much like a little sister, teasing and aggravating me when he was in our home. It was not until 1957 when he went into the Air Force after his college graduation that he told me he would like to date me. Most of our courting was done via US Mail with a few actual dates when he was on leave. The summer of 1959 he invited my family and me to come to Topeka, Kansas where he was stationed at Forbes Air Force Base. We drove out there and spent about a week with him and during that time he proposed to me and gave me an engagement ring. He knew he was going to be sent out of the country for 3 months and we decided to wait until he returned to get married.

Kenny's first civilian job took us to north central Illinois where we lived for 10 years. His employment was in the field of agriculture. During that time we had two sons, Kent and Mark, born 5 years apart. In early 1970 when Kent was 7 1/2 and Mark almost 3 we decided we wanted to move back to southern Illinois so our boys could be raised near their grandparents.

We made the move in May and lived with my parents for 5 months while our new home was being built. As we settled into the community, we started attending the church where we were married. The same one where at the age of ten I had accepted Jesus Christ as my Lord and Savior. I do not remember exactly how or when it happened but within a couple of years me, Helen Jo, our cousin, Becky, and the pastor's son, Steve, began singing together at church with Steve accompanying us on the acoustic guitar.

From the time I was born, Mom always had the radio playing and I learned to love music at a very early age. I remember listening to The Andrews Sisters, The McGuire Sisters and The Lennon Sisters as well as many male quartets, especially the Southern Gospel Quartet music of The Blackwood Brothers and The Statesmen in the 40's and 50's. I loved music, in particular the harmony of trios and quartets. Though I had sung in the church choir for many years I had never done anything with three or four-part harmony. As we began singing, Helen Jo fell into the lead part quite naturally, Becky had a wonderful alto voice, and I wound up on a higher harmony part. Steve was a natural bass.

We were enjoying singing and learning new songs and before too long other churches began inviting us to their Homecomings and other special music events. Eventually we were told by a dear friend, Wanda Farris, who encouraged and promoted us at every opportunity, "Get a name for your group and some singing clothes, you're on your way." We did as she advised, naming our group The Galatians which was taken from the book of Galatians in the New Testament simply because we liked what that book was all about. The Freedom we have in Christ as Christians. We also bought "singing clothes."

As time went by and we became better known we were traveling farther away from home. It was only natural that changes would occur in the group. Becky had to drop out for personal reasons and a friend, Cindy Parker, stepped into her place. Another change was that we now had a pianist, and bassist, to go along with Steve's acoustic guitar and when my oldest son, Kent, was fourteen he joined us as drummer. Two years after that our bass guitar player had to leave us and my youngest son, Mark, nearly eleven years old at the time, stepped into his place. We had not known that Mark was secretly learning to play the bass holed up in his room using a borrowed bass guitar. He had asked our bass player at the time for help with some of the chords, but mostly he learned by listening to bass players on some of his favorite Gospel and Country albums. Mark also credits Steve as a big influence in his learning process. Mark had been blessed with a natural talent for music, which became evident at the early age of five when he had started picking out little choruses and songs on the piano at church. By his early teens he was playing in the style of Floyd Cramer. With the addition of Mark we were almost exclusively family. Helen Jo and Steve had married in 1974. We were beginning to have serious dreams of a full-time music ministry. It was now time to think about more comfortable and economical means of transporting our personnel as well as the sound system we had purchased with money raised from yard sales.

We were quite proud of our first bus, which was a great improvement over traveling in a car following the truck with our equipment. However, compared to the awesome customized buses the bands of today travel in, ours could only be described as a redneck camper. It was a school bus, which we had a local auto body man paint white and detail with red. It looked very nice and the inside was fairly comfortable. The guys had taken out some of the seats and built bunks and closets in the back half, leaving room for the sound equipment and instruments in the very back. It had no air conditioning and no rest room.

Our second bus was a Greyhound type bus, which had air conditioning and a rest room. It was a definite improvement. The guys again customized the interior. They took out seats, built bunks and closets and made a small kitchen area. Rather than the group name on the destination sign on the front of the bus, we had GLORY BOUND. For some reason we could not keep the word BOUND fully lit and all that was visible was the "B." Therefore it was affectionately called the "GLORY B."

Finally in 1985 we had graduated to a Silver Eagle. It was larger and more comfortable and Helen Jo and I, for the first time, had our own room with a door, which afforded us a place of privacy with a measure of peace and quiet. Even though it was far from the top of the line it was a wonderful bus for us. Steve, Kent and Mark had almost completed customizing the interior by January of 1986 when we had the wreck and it was totaled.

At this point in our ministry our group had seven members. Steve Champion, my two sons Kent (23) and Mark (18), the Moore brothers, Greg (23) and Brad (15) and Helen Jo and me. We were traveling in 14 states, expanding more and more each year. We had recorded five albums and had been in the studio in November, working on the sixth. Kent, Kent and Brad or Kent and Ronny Hinson had written most of the lyrics of the songs for the new album with Mark and Kent arranging the music. We felt good about the upcoming album. Our fifth album, which had been produced by Ronny Hinson and Ronnie Drake of Nashville, TN, had been mailed out to a select number of Gospel radio stations all over the United States and 90% of the reviews from the DJs had been positive. Two or three of the songs charted. With our own songs on the sixth album and a quality production, again produced by the two Rons, we had a good chance of becoming better known throughout the entire country. It seemed we were about to realize our dream after thirteen years.

Chapter Three

I continued pleading for help to get out of the wreckage, saying over and over again how badly my legs hurt, that I did not want them to be broken and that we could not see the truck because he had no running lights. I can only imagine how terribly frustrated Steve and Kent were as they tried to help me.

A man in the first vehicle to come along after the crash relieved Brad of flagging so he could come back on the bus and help. He came to stand behind me and immediately put his hand up to support the sagging ceiling and keep it from falling down on me. He had the other hand on my shoulder and he was praying. Helen Jo returned from her trip to the back for blankets and after covering me with another one she put one hand up to the ceiling to help Brad keep it from falling. Her other hand was on my other shoulder as she prayed, "Oh, Jesus, I'm nobody and my sister needs someone. God, send one of your big angels to help my sister." As soon as the prayer was spoken I saw my legs move up and over to the left out of the wood and metal that had them pinned. They literally popped up like a cork out of a bottle. Kent, who was standing in the stairwell trying to get me out, also saw my legs move. He said it was like they were pinned one minute and the next they just moved out from under the pinning debris and were free. It was truly amazing. The debris did not move, only my legs. I told them I was out but could not walk and someone would have to help me. I had lifted myself with my hands on the arms of the chair and tried to stand up. Poor Kent was frantically trying to keep me seated because he knew there was no way I could stand. He reached for me to lift me back to the couch but as he did he blacked out and fell back onto the driver's seat. I remember asking him if he was okay. He answered that he was okay but was too weak to lift me and someone else would have to carry me to the couch. Someone called to Steve who was still outside the bus on his way to get the cheater bar. He came back on the bus the same way he had left . . . through the hole where the windshield had been. He carried me to the couch and Helen Jo covered me with blankets. I was so cold, the north wind was whistling through the whole front of the bus, which had been ripped open by the impact.

I don't know what caused Kent to black out, weakness from the sinus infection, the cessation of an adrenalin rush or the power of God's angel who came to help as Helen Jo had asked. Perhaps it was a combination of all three. As for my own personal feelings . . . I know that something *very powerful* happened in those few seconds when I was released. I believe, without a doubt, that the angel Helen Jo asked for was there and helped as she had asked. I did not see an angel, but I know he was there. I have always wished I *had* seen him.

Shortly after Steve came back on the bus and carried me to the couch, someone, I think it was Helen Jo, asked if anyone had tried the CB radio to call for help. No one had and Mark immediately went to the driver side of the bus where the CB usually sat on the dash. It was hanging outside the front of the bus and he fished it in and began calling, "Break, break, anyone out there? We've had a bad accident on I-29N at mile marker 41, we have a major injury and need an ambulance fast!" Five miles away a man with a base unit in his home picked up the call and told Mark an ambulance was on the way. We thought it remarkable that Mark got anyone at all to answer his call since the antenna had been ripped off it's mounting on the outside mirror, which was on the badly damaged door.

Several minutes had now passed and the first law enforcement official to arrive at the scene was a local county Sheriff or Deputy. He came on the bus and looked around gawking at the devastation and offering nothing in the way of assistance. He never asked if anyone was injured or said anything about help being on the way, etc. I mean no disrespect to the man, in truth he was probably young and inexperienced. However, it would not have surprised me to find out he was related to Barney Fife. Mark finally got in his face and said to him in a very stern voice, "I want to know, do you have an ambulance on the way?" To which the officer replied, "Yes, Sir!"

The second officer to arrive and come on the bus was a Missouri State Trooper. He was evidently more experienced and certainly much more professional. The ambulance arrived a few minutes after the officer who had immediately began searching for a way to get me off the bus. One of the officers started beating the left, side window across from where I was lying on the couch. He was trying to break it with his night stick. He got in several good whacks before the guys could tell him that the side windows would pop out and swing up for emergency exits. They then proceeded to show them how it was done. It would be a difficult exit for a stretcher with a woman on it, but it was the best available.

While all of the things around us were going on Helen Jo continued to try to console me and assure me that help was there and they would give me something for pain. She had also been making trips back and forth to the back of the bus collecting our purses, overnight cases, coats and anything else she thought we might need at the hospital. She wanted to be ready when the ambulance left with me because she intended to be in it too. She also got our cash box, took a little cash out to have with her, and then told Kent and Mark where it was and advised them to divide the money between all of them in case they got separated. When they had seen the ambulance arrive, they had gone back to their bunks so they would be out of the way. All the time she was doing the necessary things she was also checking on Greg and me to make sure we were still conscious and warm.

When she had made her last trip to the back Steve had followed her and told her that my left foot was severed. She asked him if it was there and he told her it was in my sock. When she told me of this exchange later she said that Steve was almost crying. As she came back up front he was telling Kent and Mark what he had told her. What a tough job he had with that conversation.

As the EMTs came on the bus Helen Jo and Brad were kneeling in the aisle beside me. All three of us were praying aloud and quite spiritedly.

I can imagine what the EMTs must have thought when they came on board and encountered out little prayer group. They got up and moved back to give the EMTs access to me so they could do their jobs. Helen Jo asked them immediately if they could give me something for pain and they assured her they would as soon as they assessed my injuries. One of the men gave Helen Jo a flashlight to hold for them since it was still dark. No one had thought to try turning on the interior lights. One of the men began to take my vital signs while the other started cutting one of the legs out of my warm up suit. At this point I don't think they suspected the seriousness of my injuries because everyone was calm and rational and there was no hysteria. Except for my continued complaints of how badly my legs were hurting, etc., everyone was quiet, only answering questions when asked.

When the EMT had my left leg exposed he realized the extent of my injuries. He took the light from Helen Jo and gave it to his partner. Helen Jo said later she thought he was probably afraid she would pass out when she saw my leg. After the EMT had my right leg and foot exposed, he found they were also in very bad condition. My injuries were probably much worse than they had expected when they had boarded the bus. They started an IV and gave me a pain shot. At this point someone finally thought to try the interior lights to see if they would turn on. They did and that was when Helen Jo got her first good look at my legs and feet. I did not see them nor did I ask about them at this point. It just never occurred to me.

After the EMTs had the IV going they began the painful process of putting my legs in Styro Splints, transferring me from the couch to the stretcher, then out the propped up window and into the ambulance. They removed the bolsters from the couch, which gave them room to roll me onto my side and slide the gurney board under me. It was very painful even with my legs in the splints. Once the board was in place they wrapped me in blankets and strapped me down. Now *that* really disturbed me! I told the EMTs that I did not want them to strap me to the stretcher but I would *let* them do it (yeah, right!) if they promised to unstrap me when they got me out of the bus. They promised they would and assured me that once in the ambulance I would be unstrapped. Being a bit claustrophobic I have never liked being held down. Strapped down is just as bad if not worse! Before they started out the window with me, Helen Jo reminded them not to leave her behind. They told her they would wait on her. I don't remember the trip out the window being scary, I do remember it took several men to accomplish the transfer. The window was a fairly narrow exit and it was a long way down from the window to the ground. I don't know if it was just the EMTs and the law enforcement officers handling the stretcher or if there were other men who had stopped to help. By this time there were a lot of vehicles and people in the median. I also noticed the traffic in the southbound lanes of the interstate. It was just crawling along, backed up as far as I could see, bumper to bumper. There was a tour bus, much like ours, on the highway even with us as they lowered me out the window. I remember wondering what they must be thinking to see a bus similar to theirs in an awful accident.

After they had me out of the bus and were carrying me toward the ambulance, Helen Jo passed our belongings out the window to one of the boys and someone helped her jump from the bus. As they loaded me in the back of the ambulance the driver told Helen Jo she could ride up front with him. When he was pulling out of the median, he pointed out the deer the truck had hit. I don't know if this was the first she knew about a deer causing the trucker to lose control of his truck and cross the median. Neither do I remember when I learned about the deer. Helen Jo asked the driver to stop so she could see the deer better. She told me later it was very torn up but she was sure it was a buck because she saw his rack. The ambulance driver apologized for having to separate our family because Greg was being taken to Heartland East Hospital, and I was going to Heartland West Hospital. He asked her questions about our group, where we were from, where we were going and kept her talking which helped her remain calm. The other EMT was in the back with me monitoring my vital signs and trying to keep me as comfortable as possible. *And* he had taken the straps off my arms just as they had promised. Both EMTs, Charlie and Mike, were wonderful.

The State Troopers had to stop traffic in the south bound lanes so the ambulance could cross into those lanes, get around the wreckage of the bus and truck, then get back into the north bound lanes toward the hospital in St. Joseph. The rest of our family had to stay with the bus until it could be towed into town. All of our personal things, sound equipment and instruments were on board and could not be left unattended.

Chapter Four

We arrived in the ER at Heartland West Hospital approximately 1 hour from the time of the crash. I believe that is called the "Golden Hour" or something like that. Meaning that if a critical patient can be gotten to the ER within that hour they have a better chance of survival. As the staff took me to be checked over Helen Jo was called in to give my statistics. Because of the extent of the injuries to my feet and legs, the ER medical team had called the orthopedic surgeon who was on call for that weekend, Dr. Jerrold Lancourt. He and his surgical assistant, Dick McLauchlin, arrived around 6:45. After he had seen me and evaluated my injuries one of the nurses went to get Helen Jo. Dr. Lancourt was introduced to her and she told him that she was my sister. After their introduction they immediately "locked horns" when he very bluntly told her, "Her right leg will have to come off above the knee and the left below the knee." She had known the situation was bad but had expected a better prognosis than what she got. It virtually threw her into a state of shock. She told him, "I can't accept that. Isn't there any alternative?" He said, "No. And there is no time for a second opinion, we have to act fast just to preserve her life. These are life threatening injuries."

At this point the gravity of the situation and responsibility thrust upon Helen Jo was nearly overwhelming and she said she remembered thinking she wished she could just pass out and escape the reality of the whole situation. However, being the tough lady she is, and never the type to pass out or buckle under in a crisis, she again challenged the doctor telling him she could not accept the amputation of my legs. She asked him if he had told me and he said he had. He had, in fact, been nearly nose-to-nose with me when he told me of the necessity of amputation and asked me, "Do you understand?" To which I had answered, "Yes." However, since I had been given pain medication, Helen Jo was the one to have to give the go-ahead and she was hanging in there for saving my legs. Dr Lancourt turned and walked away. A nurse named Hazel McGaughey got Helen Jo by the shoulders and said, "Listen, of all the orthopedic surgeons in that group who could have been on call, he is *the best*. You have been very fortunate to get him." Helen Jo told her she knew we were and she got control of herself and stopped crying. Dr. Lancourt returned to where she was standing by the gurney where I lay and it was evident he was more than a little perturbed with her. He was very stern and frank with her when he told her, "I can't be your hero. I love to do that for people but I can't for you because these are the ugliest, worst injuries of this kind I've ever seen." Later on his surgical assistant would tell my family that he had seen many such injuries in Viet Nam. It looked like I had stepped on a land mine. Dr. Lancourt made Helen Jo look at my legs and feet again. She said, "Since you've been frank and blunt with me, I will be with you. Are you a Christian?" I'd love to know what was going through his mind at this point, as he answered, "No." She then asked, "Do you go to church?" Again he answered, "No." She said, "Well, I know what I've seen and you may think I'm a religious fanatic or a holy roller or whatever, but I know the Great Physician and He's the Lord Jesus Christ. I'm believing He's going to intervene. I'm believing for a miracle and I will be praying for you." Dr. Lancourt said, "Yes, there are lots of kinds of miracles and right now just saving her life will be one." Helen Jo said, "I realize that and can accept it but I am still believing for a miracle and I will be praying for you." Dr. Lancourt said, "I will tell you one thing, I'm going to save as much tissue as possible." She said, "That's all I wanted to hear. God bless you." As the doctor and his assistant left to prepare for surgery a sweet and compassionate nurse named, Cheryl Gilgore, hugged Helen Jo and told her, "That's all right, honey, I'm one (a religious fanatic) too." Cheryl had come to me, while the doctor and Helen Jo were talking, and told me they had a prayer chain at her church. She asked me if I would like for her to call them and I said, "Oh, yes, please do." She smiled and said, "I already have, and I just wanted you to know." She was such a comfort to us, especially Helen Jo for she gave her a shoulder to cry on which she so badly needed. It was also wonderful to know someone of the same faith was there with us.

I was given an injection just before they wheeled me to the elevator on my way to the surgical suite. Helen Jo came to the head of the gurney to talk to me before I was taken away and I told her, "Helen Jo, leave it in the hands of the Lord. Remember that song we were talking about on the bus as we were leaving last night, *Don't Give Up On the Brink of Your Miracle?*" She said, "That's right, and we're not going to."

I understood what might have to be done and I also knew the terrible responsibility, which had been thrust upon her. I was truly in God's hands whatever the outcome but I feel certain He used Helen Jo in a special way that morning. She had "stood in the gap" for me against a very competent doctor who was only wanting to do his job as he thought best . . . a doctor we would come to love very dearly in spite of his stern way of speaking in that clipped New York accent.

Around 7:00 AM after I had been taken to surgery, Helen Jo asked for a phone to call home. She decided to call my husband first and have him call Dad and Mom. Then she called our pastor, Rev. James Drysdale. She knew we needed prayer and that was the best place to begin. When she talked with my husband he assured her he would be there as soon as possible. She was taken to the nurse's lounge by two of the ER nurses to wait while I was in surgery. They did not want to send her to a big waiting room to wait all by herself. They also called the hospital's Chaplin and he came to be with her. She then requested that someone go and get Kent or have a State Trooper bring him to the hospital so she would have a family member there with her. He arrived at 7:30 AM and was told about my condition. Still very ill from the sinus infection, he immediately asked where to find the nearest restroom. He was back and forth to the restroom for the next hour and a half until the Chaplin went to find crackers and 7-Up for him. Finally something to settle his stomach and help him to feel better. He also lay down for a little while. When he was feeling better he asked more about the extent of my injuries and the course of action the doctor was taking. One of the first questions he asked Helen Jo was which foot was gone. When she told him the left one he said, "Good, she can still drive." Of course, I first had to survive surgery.

Chapter Five

In all the years we had been traveling, spreading the Gospel in song and testimony, we had many interesting, inspiring and comical situations come our way. The majority of the people we met were wonderful and loving. We worked with many other groups. Local groups, who like us, were virtually unknown outside of our own tri-state area. We also worked with nationally known groups such as The Goodman Family, The Easter Brothers, The Hinson Family, Wendy Bagwell & the Sunlighters and Gold City Quartet, to name a few. Many became friends and were in and out of our home for food, showers, etc. when in our area. We opened concerts for all of them at one time or another.

One young family group we met early on, probably around 1976, was the Robinson Family, also from southern, IL. Al, Darlene, LaShanda, Greg & Geinger. Little did we know when we met them for the first time that five year old Geinger would marry our youngest son, Mark, in July of 1993. Seven years later they would give us our first grandchild, Jacob Gregory, and almost six years after his arrival came his little brother, Ethan Kent. What a joy they are to us!

Also early in our career we met a local Gospel disk jockey, Rev. Dean Stevenson who gave Mark the nickname of, "The Smallest Bass Player in the World." He was always small for his age and when he started playing the bass guitar for the group at the age of eleven, he was so small he could not hold the 3/4 size bass guitar for an entire concert. He sat perched on a step stool. Everybody fell in love with him and came to concerts just to see that cute little boy play the bass. Our young band seemed to appeal to people of all ages.

Our experiences in the different venues were many and varied. Such as the time in a small country church in Texas when the men were carrying in the sound equipment and instruments and the double front doors, frame and all, came forward and fell toward them as they opened the door. They had to put it back together before they could carry in the first piece of equipment. In that same church one young man arrived late and came straight to the platform, where we were already into our first song, plugged in his electric guitar and started playing along with the band. Not a bad thing unless the musician plays everything in the key of C. After the first song he apologized for being late and continued to play the entire concert along with our band. Much to the band's credit, they handled it with grace and continued to discreetly turn up our sound system to try to over ride the out-of-sync accompaniment. There was one thing that *did* impress our band at that church though . . . the rear view mirror on the old upright piano. Our pianist thought it very cool to be able to see everything that was going on behind him!

Another small country church in Georgia presented a very different kind of challenge to one of the young men in our band. When we took a mid-concert break a young woman, 15 or 16 years old, gave me a note for Kent. I figured it was a fan note about how much she liked him, etc. but I was wrong. I passed the note to Kent and though I don't know exactly what the note said, the gist of it was that she had been contemplating suicide. Something about watching the young people in the band and our group had made her have second thoughts and she wanted to talk with Kent. Kent talked with her and counseled her and she left with a better perspective on her life. To our knowledge she never carried through with the suicide she had contemplated. I personally corresponded with her for 2 or 3 years before we finally lost touch. It is my hope that she went on to live a happy and blessed Christian life.

We worked with many pastors and evangelists through the years. One of the most interesting and dynamic evangelists we ever worked with was an Assembly of God preacher, Rev. Billy Martin. His family traveled with him and sang and played instruments much like ours. His son, Aaron, and daughter, Bonnita, were around the same age as our boys and they all hit it off wonderfully. They enjoyed making music together before, during or after concerts, it made no difference, they all loved music. Bonnita and Aaron had written a silly song called "Fried Ham," inspired by all of the ham they had been served at churches through the years while on the evangelistic field. It was silly and corny and fun! Bro. Martin was a big barrel-chested man who enjoyed roughhousing with the boys and aggravating them. He wore his dark hair in a pompadour, all slicked back, every hair in place. And, oh, how Kent loved to mess up that head of hair! Which he did at every opportunity. Opening for Bro. Martin was one of our favorite venues. One of the most memorable times was when Bro. Martin came into the church a few minutes before time for the service to begin wearing a canary yellow suit. Our boys cracked up to see him all decked out in that bright yellow suit. The service had just started when I noticed that the guys of the band were sitting about 3 rows back from the front of the church, which was highly unusual. It was not unusual for me and Helen Jo to sit that close to the front, however, the men generally preferred to stand in the back of the church until time to take their places on the platform. When Bro. Martin came to the pulpit he took one look at them and said, "Okay boys, stand up and turn around!" All of them had on sunglasses. The whole congregation, as well as Bro. Martin, roared with laughter as the guys took a bow!

We were treated to many sermons throughout the years. Most were good and interesting, even entertaining. However, enduring the preaching of the "Billy Goat Preacher" was difficult for all of us. No joke, he sounded just like a Billy goat when he got going. I had never heard anything quite like it in my life. As the oldest member of the group, mother of two of the boys, and substitute mom for the others while on the road, it was my job to keep them "in line," although it was seldom necessary. This particular night I had an uneasy feeling about their reaction to the unusual preaching style. Helen Jo and I were sitting near the front of the church, a couple of pews back. I knew the boys were standing or sitting in the back somewhere. I felt like I needed to check on them and make sure they were not doing anything they should not be doing. When I finally got a chance to turn around and check on them they were standing like perfect gentlemen with straight faces and admirable composure. I could hardly believe it. I was very proud of them because it was difficult for me to keep from laughing out loud when the preacher would take off again on a long Billy goat rant.

Some of the experiences we had never involved anybody but our own group. A couple of them could have been tragic. We were in Georgia one time, on our way to a concert when we decided to stop for the night at an RV campground Steve had seen advertised on a billboard. He made the turn he thought would lead to the camp site and after slowly easing up a hill with one lane for what seemed like miles he decided it was not the right road. He eased up a little further and the road got narrower and steeper until it was evident it was not leading anywhere we should be going. And the worst part was there was no place to turn around. He had to back down the hill we had just gone up, in the dark. If I remember correctly Kent and Mark were out of the bus trying to direct Steve and Brad was hanging out the door watching them and relaying their instructions to Steve the best he could. Helen Jo and I were in our bunks in the back praying and pleading the blood of Jesus over us, the bus and anything else we thought needed it. Greg was doing his usual prayer, which consisted of, "Jesus, Jesus, Jesus!" Over and over. It had to be God answering our prayers that got us down that narrow steep road on that pitch black night. We laughed about it later but it was definitely not a funny situation at the time.

One other time, I think we were in Arkansas where we had sung at a church Homecoming that afternoon. Helen Jo and I were on the bus in our room changing our clothes while the guys took care of the taking down and loading of the equipment. Steve had come on the bus and started it but had not yet moved it to the front of the church where they could load the equipment into the bays. He got off the bus and started back to the church when he heard it start moving. Somehow it had jumped into gear and was backing toward a hill. Helen Jo and I never thought anything about it moving because we knew it had been started and just thought it was being moved to the church. When Steve realized what was happening, he took off in a dead run for the door of the bus, which thankfully he had left open. He managed to get in the driver seat and get it stopped just before it got to the edge of the drop-off. When he got out and saw how close it was and what was below the hill it was even scarier. I don't know how high the hill was but many feet below us there was a cemetery. As in many of our experiences we managed to find the humor in it and laughed about how Helen Jo and I very nearly wound up in the cemetery that day. Literally!

We loved what we were doing, although it was hard work with little sleep and, sometimes, even less pay. Many times, not even getting enough of a "love offering" to buy diesel for the bus and food for the seven people in the group. We knew that one of the things we needed to do was write and sing our own music. By 1984 our band had begun writing songs. Kent was good with lyrics and was writing at every opportunity on his own as well as with Brad and Ronny Hinson. Ronny was already a very prolific and experienced songwriter and a very good mentor for Kent. Mark was good at arranging the music after the songs were written. Our sixth album would have featured many of their songs. Three or four of those songs were already recorded in Nashville at Hilltop Studio and we were due back in the studio in Feb. of 1986 to complete the project. Unfortunately, due to our accident, that never happened and the songs we had already recorded were lost.

Chapter Six

At home in Olive Branch, my husband began making phone calls. First to Dad and Mom, which had to be the most difficult one. He then called our place of business, a John Deere dealership, and let them know what had happened. He also knew he would need a larger vehicle than our car or pick up truck to get everyone home as well as the equipment, etc. He called a friend, explained the situation, and asked to borrow his van. He threw his clothes in a bag and set out to meet the friend with the van and switch our vehicle for his. He was then on his way on the eight hour trip to St. Joseph not knowing exactly what he would find when he got there. Our parents could not make the trip that day because they were keeping Helen Jo and Steve's three year old son, Matthew, and would have to make arrangements for his care before they could leave. It would be the next day, Sunday before they could get away.

Greg had been checked over at Heartland East and found to have badly bruised knees and hands. He also had glass particles in the backs of his hands. Thank God his physical injuries were not as serious as mine. He had requested to be reunited with the rest of our group and arrived at Heartland West at 9:30 AM. He asked someone to help him find Helen Jo. They contacted her and she went to find him and take him to the nurse's lounge where she and Kent were waiting. When he was told of my injuries he fell into Helen Jo's arms crying and apologizing as if the accident and my injuries were his fault. She consoled him and assured him that it was not his fault and no one could have done any better. Not long after Greg was reunited with Helen Jo and Kent an insurance agent from the trucking firm came to get a statement from him and his account of the accident. It was upsetting to him to have to go over the whole thing again and relive it, so to speak. After the agent left Helen Jo suggested he call his older brother, Nick, and have him go and tell their mother, Carolyn, about the accident. Nick was not at home but his wife, Lisa, took the call and said she would go to Carolyn's place of business and tell her.

While Greg had been making the call home Helen Jo had gone to try and find out how the surgery was going. She found Cheryl and asked her if she could check for her. Cheryl called the surgery suite and talked with one of the nurses. After the call she reported that they were half way through with the surgery and she said, "I don't want to give you false hope, but there were no major arteries or vessels severed." That really sounded good to Helen Jo and she went back to the lounge and told Kent. She also told him she figured it would be at least two hours from then before they would know any more. Kent was finally feeling better, at least his stomach was settled and he was no longer nauseous. Greg returned from making his call and the three of them settled in for more waiting.

At 11:00 AM a nurse from the operating room called down and told them I was out of surgery and in the recovery room. Helen Jo said she really had mixed feelings about it. On the one hand she was glad I was out of surgery but on the other she was almost afraid to learn what the doctor had done. She was especially concerned about my right leg. However, she did not think they would have had time to do anything as radical as amputation.

While they were waiting for Dr. Lancourt to come and give his report of the surgery, Steve arrived. He had been separated from Mark and Brad, who were left with the bus at the salvage yard, while he went to try and find a rental trailer for our equipment and personal belongings. After checking on rental trailers he had not gone back to the salvage yard to pick them up. They immediately began to make arrangements to have them picked up, only to discover that they had already been brought from the salvage yard and were somewhere in the hospital. Somehow they located them and had them come to the lounge where they were waiting. For the first time in five or six hours they were all together again. There was bound to be a great deal of comfort in that.

It was another hour before Dr. Lancourt and his assistant Dick arrived to tell them what all had been done in surgery. Helen Jo said her stomach ached and she felt sick all over when she saw them coming. Dr. Lancourt told them first of all that I had, "Zonked" on them as they started to put me to sleep. My blood pressure had hit bottom and they had to start pumping blood into the artery in my neck. I was a bit more than a quart low! (My comment, not the doctor's.) He explained that they had completed the amputation of my left foot at the ankle because it was crushed and mangled too badly to repair. He said, "There just wasn't a foot there to reconstruct." Both bones in both legs were broken or crushed. The compound fracture of the left tibia had caused a nasty open wound on my shin. The leg and stump were cleaned up and packed with Betadine soaked gauze. My right leg had been cleaned up and the huge eight or ten inch wound on the back of my leg, that he said he could stick his hand down in, had been packed with Betadine soaked gauze. The other open wound on my shin was six or eight inches long and fairly deep. The right tibia, also a compound fracture, had a 1" gap in the bone where it had been crushed to powder. Half of my right foot had been amputated because it, too, was beyond repair and my right ankle was broken. Dr. Lancourt said they were taking a wait-and-see attitude, especially about the right leg. They had not set any of the broken bones. He said that for the next little while it would be back to surgery every three or four days to take a look, clean up, etc. Everyone was relieved they had not taken the right leg off although he said that it was still a possibility and could mean above the knee just as he had told us initially. He went on to say that my injuries were still life threatening and my whole system had been traumatized. I needed to have good circulation in both limbs. He told them my enemies were infection, blood clots and debris in the blood. For the time being, he had stopped the bleeding and I was stable. Injuries, other than my legs and feet, were superficial. I had a knot on my forehead and several little cuts on my face and the backs of my hands from the flying glass. I would be in the recovery room for a couple of hours. From there I would be taken to ICU. My family was taken to a waiting area known as "The Bridge" to wait until I was in ICU and they could see me. They were facing another long wait. During their wait the guys began to talk about going back to the bus to collect personal clothing and toilet articles they would need in the coming days.

After a couple of hours they were told I was in ICU and they could see me. I asked about Kenny. He has always been my rock and I have known I could trust his judgment and level headedness to know what to do in any situation. I wanted him there in the worst way, for myself as well as for Helen Jo and our boys. I continued to ask for him that afternoon and evening. Helen Jo kept assuring me he was on his way and would be there that night.

The Chaplin from the Pastoral Care Department of the hospital had stayed with my family during my surgery. He was a great help to them during that time. He had secured rooms for them in the hospital just down the hall from ICU. Any member of my family could come down the hall to see me any time they wanted, day or night. The only restriction was that they not wake me up if I was sleeping. These rooms, set aside for family, were called, "Stay Inns." The hospital rented them, at a very reasonable rate to families such as mine, who were far from home with a loved one in critical condition in the hospital. And it was good for all of us that they could be so close to me in ICU. This was a new program the hospital had just begun and wonderful for my family.

After they saw me in ICU they were taken to their rooms where they settled in. They were immediately greeted by constantly ringing phones. Our family in southern Illinois, as well as Greg and Brad's family in southeast Missouri and friends from all over the country were calling as they got news of the accident. Evidently the news had spread very rapidly because the hospital switchboard had been jammed with calls. They recruited the security guards to help answer the phones until they could make arrangements for a couple of lines directly to my families rooms for the incoming calls. Between calls they managed to get showers and clean up and then went to the cafeteria to eat. After eating they tried to nap. Helen Jo was making frequent trips to the ICU to check on me.

What a horribly long and traumatic day for everyone, it seemed to have no end. They were very glad to see Kenny when he arrived around 7:00 PM. Upon his arrival they finally had someone to lean on and make decisions. Helen Jo would no longer have the full responsibility of decisions about me all on her shoulders. They brought him to where I was in ICU and I was so glad to see him. I can only imagine how he felt seeing me for the first time in the condition I was in, but what a relief it was to have him with me at last.

Steve's parents arrived in Olive Branch that night at midnight to take care of Matthew. Mom and Daddy would leave Sunday morning to drive to St. Joseph. I am sure everyone was a little concerned about Daddy driving all that distance to St. Joseph. He could always get lost on the highways faster than anybody we ever knew; he has absolutely no sense of direction. We have always affectionately called him, "Wrong-way Corrigan." Put him in the woods squirrel hunting and he had no trouble whatsoever finding his way around, but on the highway, if he could make a wrong turn he would!

PART TWO

Heartland West Hospital— St. Joseph, MO

January 26th, day 2.

My second day in ICU my period started. It was surely brought on by the trauma because it was not time for it. Regardless, it was another test of my modesty, dignity and endurance because the nurses had to take care of that for me too. And, of course, moving my body for any reason caused me more pain than I was already in. Before the bones in my legs were set, my family said they could hear them grating together when my legs were moved. They were so swollen they looked like they might burst and perhaps that was a possibility. The nurses were measuring them every day, monitoring the swelling. Every time they would come in to slip the measuring tape around my thighs it would hurt something awful and I dreaded it every time. They would gently lift my legs and slide the tape under, but it was still excruciating. And because of the constant pain I never totally relaxed even with pain medication. I was holding my body very tense and rigid. Although I was kept heavily medicated I was never totally pain free.

My nurses, Barbara Tunks and Mary Schmitt, were concerned about more than the condition of my legs. My hair was absolutely full of powdery glass and since my warm-up suit had been covered with it too, when it was cut away the glass went everywhere. I remember hearing them talk about how to get the glass out of my hair and especially out of my belly button. It seemed Barb was most concerned with that. As soon as I felt like it, and

I don't remember when that was, Mary put a towel under my head and gently brushed my hair trying to rid it of the glass. Barb was on a mission to deglass my belly button and had an idea that a cotton swab dipped in Vaseline might do the job of collecting the glass. It worked beautifully and she was ecstatic!

Helen Jo was in and out the first day and night and came in early the second morning. After she had checked on me she went back to her room to dress and put her make-up on. When she was walking back to my room she met Dr. Lancourt in the hall and it was evident he did not recognize her. He pointed his finger at her and said, "You're the sister." Her eyes were not as swollen nor her nose as red as they had been the day before from all the tears she had shed. With her make-up on and jeans and a sweater rather than her old blue warm-up suit and white rabbit coat, she truly did look much different. They spoke and then he got right to the point. For the first time he said he would try to save my right leg. I would have surgery the next day, Monday, to place Hoffman pins in each leg to set the bones. It would also involve cleaning up the tissue (debridement) and repacking the open wounds and wrapping them with gauze. This would be the procedure for the next few weeks, as I went back to surgery every three or four days. Though the doctor made no promises, he seemed a little more optimistic. Helen Jo told him we appreciated him and all he was doing and that we loved him.

Kenny came in just after Dr. Lancourt left so Helen Jo filled him in on what the doctor had said and then they went on down to the cafeteria to eat. They had learned before they left their rooms that Mom and Daddy were on their way. Had I been a bit more aware of all that was going on I would have been concerned about our folk's trip to St. Joe. Daddy would have to get around St. Louis as well as Kansas City and then find his way to the hospital. With his record of wrong turns no telling where they would wind up.

Around 9:30 the boys were up and ready to eat. They met up with Kenny and Helen Jo and they proceeded to tell them the news about my legs and the upcoming surgery on Monday. After they had eaten they set out to try to rent a trailer to haul our sound equipment back to Olive Branch. The problem was money. They did not have enough to rent the size they would need.

Gaylen and Judy Rainforth, and three other people from one of the churches where we were booked in Nebraska, came to visit, arriving around noon. When we were singing at their church in Hastings, it was always Gaylen and Judy's house where we parked the bus. They gave us the run of their home, fed us royally and gave us access to their bathroom. Although we had a small bathroom on the bus we did not have a shower. In general they took very good care of us and through the years we had become good friends. They had driven several hours just to visit and be with us. Judy felt terrible about the wreck, as she was the one who had booked us into their church as she always did. She also knew how much we ladies loved our pretty high-heeled shoes and it really bothered her that I would probably never be able to wear them again. They stayed two or three hours before making the long drive back to their home.

At 3:30 that afternoon the wife of Pastor Brown from First Assembly of God Church came to ICU with a check for the amount we needed for the rental of the trailer. Helen Jo had contacted the pastor earlier and told him of our need and his church took care of it. The pastor's wife also told us that if we needed *anything* else to call them. Wow, what a wonderful church. We had never sung there and they did not know us from Adam, but they met our need without a question.

With the check from the First Assembly of God Church in hand, the guys started out for the rental place. The bus had to be stripped. All of our personal belongings, and anything salvageable, had to be removed and transported home. It was a gruesome job. Somehow Kent got the job of removing mine and Helen Jo's clothing and shoes from our room. He told me later that it really bothered him when he packed up my shoes . . . several boxes of pretty high-heeled shoes I wore with my stage dresses. By 6:00 PM they had removed everything from the bus and packed it into the trailer. They returned to the hospital bringing in everything they thought might be needed for our stay. They also came in to ICU to say their goodbyes to me. I really hated to see them leave and their parting left me with a lonely feeling, even though Helen Jo and Kenny were still there and Mom and Dad would soon be arriving. I knew it was important they return home to take care of things there but deep down inside I wanted all of my people around me and did not want them to leave. It was a sad parting and there were many tears.

Dad and Mom arrived shortly after Steve, Kent, Mark, Greg and Brad had left. They had made good time and for once Daddy did not get lost. I was very glad to see them and I remember telling Mom that I had lost something that I would never get back. Meaning my feet. After they visited with me for a little while then went in search of Helen Jo. Throughout the evening everyone tried to rest as much as possible. They were taking turns sitting with me. We were all anxious to hear from the guys as soon as they arrived home. At 3:00 AM they called to say they were home safe and sound.

Monday January 27th, day three.

Helen Jo was down to check on me by 6:00 AM as usual then went back to her room to dress and then have breakfast in the cafeteria. The day's surgery was on everyone's mind and they were anxious for it to be over. The nurse told them they would probably come for me at 1:00. At 12:30 they came in to give me an injection. Kenny, Helen Jo and Daddy and Mom were with me until they came to take me to surgery. They went to eat lunch and begin the long wait. While I was in surgery the head of the REHAB department had come by the waiting room to talk with Helen Jo. She left literature for her to read about prosthetics, etc. Later on Helen Jo told me it had encouraged her to learn of the rehabilitation and prosthetics available for people with losses like mine. As she shared what she had learned I listened but I did not really want to hear it or think about what the future held for me. I was not in denial; I just was not ready to think about it yet.

At 4:00 PM they still had not heard anything from surgery and Helen Jo asked someone to call and ask if I was still in the operating room. The report was that they were almost finished and the family was to go down to the ICU family waiting room. It was only minutes until they saw Dr. Lancourt and his assistant, Dick. The doctor stated that he had done exactly what he had set out to do. They put two Hoffman pins in the left leg and trimmed off more of the foot area so that they could make me a nice flap for my prosthetic fitting later on. He had saved my heel pad, from the bottom of my foot, which was still attached to my leg. If it remained healthy it would be used to cover the bottom of the stump. That's what he had meant by a "nice flap." They put three pins in the right leg, a much more complicated leg to deal with because of the large open wounds. Because of the one-inch gap in the tibia bone he was not sure it would heal. He said, "Might heal . . . might not." The doctor said there was a pulse in the remaining half of my right foot, and it was healthy and healing well. They had put a screw in the broken anklebone. He said they had accomplished a lot in the surgery. They would take a look the next day and see how my legs were doing. Hopefully I would continue doing well. The prayer chain would have something specific to pray about when they called to check that night.

Kenny introduced Dr. Lancourt to Mom and Daddy. Helen Jo told him she appreciated him and all he had done and she just had to give him a hug. He willingly received it and said he could take a lot of those hugs. She told him she loved him and then Mom hugged him too, thanked him and cried. Dr. Lancourt's assistant had gone to answer a call and when he returned the doctor made sure Dick knew he had gotten hugs! Of course, that meant Helen Jo and Mom had to give Dick hugs too.

Around 5:00 PM my family went to eat dinner and then spend some time answering the phones. After I was returned to my cubicle in ICU they came to see me. Helen Jo got to talk with the nurse, Barbara, who was as happy and pleased with the outcome of the surgery as the family was. She told Helen Jo that Dr. Lancourt had been very excited to find the pulse in my foot. She showed them my legs and they decided they looked a little like a Sputnik with the pins sticking out several inches and the external braces holding them together. According to the entry in Helen Jo's journal, they looked great to her. They were still very swollen and battered, but under the circumstances they looked great.

While Helen Jo was talking with Barbara, Dr. Lancourt called. She overheard Barbara's side of the conversation and could tell that the doctor was thrilled. He asked Barbara didn't she think my family was a nice family and she said, "Yes, they are." He then asked her if she thought they were pleased with everything and she told him, "Oh, yes, and so am I!" After she hung up the phone she shared the doctor's part of the conversation with Helen Jo confirming what she thought was being said. Then Helen Jo told Barbara about butting heads with Dr. Lancourt in the ER. Barbara told her she had done the right thing. She had every right to want to save that tissue and to fight for it.

Daddy wanted to stay with me that night and they allowed him to sit in a chair by the bed. I knew he was there and was doing a lot of praying and that was a comfort to me. I slept a lot because of the anesthetic in surgery as well as the pain medication. However, I was never out of pain! The medication dulled it a bit, but it was always there. My family said they did notice that after the bones were set I was no longer as tense and rigid against the pain. I had visibly relaxed for the first time.

Tuesday January 28th, day four.

Helen Jo's 31st birthday. What a way to spend a birthday! She was down to see me around 6:00 AM, as she had been the previous days. I remember feeling bad because she had to celebrate her birthday in the hospital. Our family has always been big on birthday parties with cake, ice cream and presents and she was not getting hers. I'm sure everyone else would have enjoyed it but I was not ready for cake and ice cream just yet. The only thing that was at all appealing to me was 7-Up. Wonderful stuff, 7-Up!

At 10:15 the doctor and his assistant were in to check on me. Dr. Lancourt wanted Kenny and Helen Jo to see his handiwork and showed them the pins and braces. They agreed with him that everything looked great. I took their word for it for I still had not seen my legs nor did I care to at that time. Just feeling them was bad enough. I knew they were huge from the swelling which seemed to have stopped but had not gone down. I could still feel both feet and my toes were burning something awful. My right foot felt like it was bound very tightly and bandaged with the toes turned under. Phantom pains, it's called. My legs continued to be in a lot of pain although not as intense since the pins had been put in place to hold the bones together. I was trying not to tense up as much and manage the pain a little better. However, I thought I had developed a hemorrhoid and told the nurse. Sure enough, holding my body so tense and rigid and bearing down from the pain had caused one to form. I was one big mess of hurt from the waist down. I just wanted them to keep the pain medication coming and add some Preparation H to the list!

Around 7:00 PM the phones started ringing for updates on my condition and what people needed to pray about. It usually took all of the family to field the calls and give the updated reports. Also during this time the Pastor of a Baptist Church near St. Joseph came by. He was a friend of the Pastor of First Southern Baptist Church in Cairo, IL, a town near our home where a lot of relatives and friends lived. The pastor from Cairo had called him and asked him to come to the hospital and check on us. He visited for a short time and prayed with us. It was another example of the love and concern of people all around . . . both near and far away.

Wednesday January 29th, day 5.

The trauma of the wreck and my injuries, as well as the loss of sleep the last five days, had taken a toll on Helen Jo and she had been urged by Mom and Daddy to sleep later if she could and try to catch up on her rest. Rather than her usual visit around 6:00 or 7:00 she arrived at 9:00. Kenny, Mom and Daddy came earlier and checked on me and visited. I was in a lot of pain and it seemed the morphine was not doing the job as well as it had been. They talked with the nurse about it and she agreed that my body was getting accustomed to it. The doctor instructed her to add Demerol to my medication. They would begin by giving it every three hours with Morphine in between. That did help to ease the pain.

Mr. Murle Black, the father of the ER nurse Cheryl, came that day and took Kenny and Helen Jo out to lunch. It's amazing how wonderful the people were to us. It seemed they could not do enough to help us or try to make things easier for my family. I think it was that same day that Kenny remembered that an associate from a previous job lived in St. Joseph and he called him. When Dick learned of the accident and my injuries, he and his wife offered their home to my family any time they wanted or needed to get away from the hospital. Dixie, Dick's wife, came and picked up my family's laundry and did it for them the whole time we were in town. They were just as wonderful as I remembered them being when Kenny had worked with Dick 20+ years earlier.

Dr. Lancourt came in at 12:30. He was still there when Helen Jo came for one of her routine checks on me. For the first time he actually sat and visited with us. He asked about the accident and how I was trapped. I suppose it was the first time he really knew what had happened to cause the injuries he was working so hard to repair and help heal. It turned out he was a very nice man along with being the best Orthopedic Surgeon in town. And, although he had said he could not be Helen Jo's hero that first morning in the ER, I think he came pretty close.

After Helen Jo returned to her room she had a call from Ronny Hinson. We had opened concerts for his family group, The Hinsons, several times, the most recent being just two or three weeks before the accident. He and Kent had also been writing songs together and he and his partner Ronnie Drake were producing our sixth album. He wanted to know all about the wreck and my injuries. He encouraged Helen Jo and told her to tell me he planned to see me walking and singing again. He also said he wanted to talk with me as soon as I was in my own room with a phone.

I had begun to finally rest better after the bones were set and the change in the pain medication. There were now periods when I was nearly pain free for a time. However, I was beginning to have silly dreams. One of the nurses told my family that Demerol would make a person dream. In her words, "You'll have Oz, Dorothy, Toto and the whole bit." My dreams were not along that line though. One of the most vivid dreams I had was of fried potatoes. They were running through my mind on a "ticker tape" like the old machines reporting the stock market used to kick out. Now days it's seen on television as a "crawler" across the bottom of the screen reporting stock market numbers, news bulletins and weather warnings. As the potatoes were running across my mind on the crawler, I would reach out and try to pick them off. My family did not know what I was reaching for and would take my hands and hold them. When I awoke after that dream and they asked me what I was reaching for I told them and we all laughed about it. One of my nurses said she wanted to go home and fry up a big skillet of potatoes for me. Of course, at that time I could not have eaten them if she had. I had just been given the go-ahead for a liquid diet. That night when they brought a cup of beef broth it tasted good to me and I drank all of it. Not fried potatoes, but the first nourishment other than 7-Up since we left Illinois on the night of the 24th

During the 3 weeks I was in Heartland West Hospital we had several visitors. Many were friends and some were strangers. People who were concerned after hearing or reading about the wreck and my injuries, or people who wanted to help and just let us know they were praying. We were always surprised at their kindness at offering to open their homes to people they did not know.

Two of the strangers who came to visit were extra special. One was a sweet lady in a red coat named Alice Sutton. She said she had read about our accident and my injuries and realized we were the same age. It just broke her heart and she had to come and see me. She asked if there was anything she could do and she offered her home to my family as a place to stay if they needed it. She also offered to feed them. She was rather shy, very humble and sweet. She reminded us of my dad's cousin, Dodie. They had the same shy and humble spirits. After her first visit we always referred to her as Dodie's proxy. They were just so very much alike.

Sometime in the third week I was in Heartland another special visitor showed up. He was a sweet man in overalls whose wife had had surgery and was in the room across the hall from me on the third floor. He too had read about the accident and when he realized I was across the hall from his wife, he said he had to come and ask if there was anything he could do. He wanted me to know how sorry he was that I had been so badly injured and he seemed especially sorry about the loss of my feet. His sweet spirit reminded me so much of our dear friend, Elisha Jordan in Georgia. We had met him at an outdoor concert one night a year or so before. I remember standing on the flatbed of a truck singing under a big light and the bugs nearly carrying us off they were so thick. And there stood Elisha under another light across the yard from where we were on the truck. He had such a sweet smile I focused on him and sang to him a lot. When we finished our part of the concert and were walking back to the bus he came and introduced himself and told us he had lived in Illinois for a time. We chatted for a while and really hit it off. He was about the age of our dad. The man in overalls at the hospital and Elisha were so much alike it was as uncanny as the likeness of the two women, Alice and Dodie. Elisha always wore a long sleeved shirt with his overalls and so did the man at the hospital and both men had the same humble and compassionate spirit about them. I regret that we never got the name of the man in overalls because he had become Elisha's proxy to us. God does work in mysterious ways. I have no doubt He could send people who could, and would, fill in for others who cared so much about us and could not get to us.

Each evening between 6:00 and 9:00 my family continued to answer many calls. They always gave updates on my condition and told the people specifically what to pray about. I have often wondered just how long the prayer chain for me was. It must have been very long with some very powerful prayer warriors on it because I was already such a miracle. I was almost into day 6 and there was no infection, no blood clots and no debris in the blood. Praise the Lord! Those were the three enemies Dr. Lancourt had warned my family about.

Thursday January 30th, day 6.

After the dream about fried potatoes, I began to complain about the liquid diet and wanted "real food." Fried potatoes were at the top of the list but not an option at that time.

For the second day Helen Jo did not come to check on me quite as early. Mom and Dad had encouraged her to rest a little longer and try to catch up on some of the sleep she had lost over the last several days. Everyone began to relax a little as my condition remained stable, with none of the complications the doctor had mentioned initially, and the pain was a bit more under control. However, the stress was beginning to catch up, especially with Helen Jo.

Once again Mr. Black came to the hospital to take my family out for lunch and to take them shopping for necessities. Kenny chose to remain with me, and I was glad of that. Helen Jo, Mom and Daddy went with Mr. Black. He first took them to a department store to find a gown and robe for me then to Wal-Mart for shampoo, etc. When we were on tour we only traveled with enough clothing and personal necessities for the three or four days we would be away. Thanks to Greg's habit and mine of over packing for each outing Helen Jo had enjoyed a little variety in clothing borrowing from our closets. However, she was to the point where she needed to purchase a few things of her own as well as things for the guys.

When they returned from the shopping trip they learned that two things had occurred while they were away. First, the insurance people had been there to take a statement from me. As it had been with Greg, it was upsetting for me to have to talk about the accident and relive it. It was the first time I had cried about it. Kenny was there with me, thank God, and that helped a lot but it was still an ordeal. It took me all the rest of that day to get over the recounting of the accident for the insurance people.

Second, Dr. Lancourt had been in to see me and told us they would change the bandages on my legs the next day. He told us the approximate time so that anyone in the family who wanted to see my legs could be there. He also said he had tentatively scheduled surgery for the next Tuesday. Again it would be for debridement and clean up of the wounds.

We were all anxious to know how Greg was doing so Helen Jo called him at home. He said his legs were bothering him quite a bit. Helen Jo encouraged him to go have them checked again to see what was going on and be sure nothing had been missed in the exam at the hospital in St. Joseph. He told her that he, Brad and their mother, Carolyn, were coming to St. Joseph to see me on Saturday.

Helen Jo also talked with Steve and Matt at home and Matt informed his mother that his dad was starving him to death! He said they only had turkey hot dogs and one slice of bologna. She figured that was Matt's three-year-old way of getting even with her for being gone so long and not there with him. In short, he missed his mama and he was hungry for real food!!

Helen Jo and Mom were finally able to take a little time for themselves to get baths and wash their hair. When any of them were in their rooms for any length of time they were answering the phones or making calls. One person who called every night for a report was our good friend Sandy Stevenson, wife of Rev. Dean Stevenson. She was very upset about what had happened and wanted so badly to get to us. However, distance and other obligations kept her at home. She was one of many who felt that way and were in touch daily or every few days. Everyone wanted updates on my condition and to know what to pray specifically for. I had a wonderful and incredibly large bunch of people loving me and praying for me.

After Helen Jo was all bathed and spiffed up she came down to my room to sit with me for a while and relieve Kenny. Earlier that day Dr. Lancourt had decided I could use one more unit of blood, which they started administering that evening. I had done fine with the first half unit but when they started the second half I had a bad reaction. My temperature shot up and I began having chills. They immediately stopped the blood and closely monitored my vital signs. When the chills stopped I started having hot flashes and sweating. One of the nurses explained that the temperature and resulting chills was my body's way of fighting something in the blood that did not agree with my system. The hot flashes and sweating was a good sign that my fever was coming down. It made me feel better to understand what was going on, but it had given everyone a bit of a scare, especially the three young nurses who were on the night shift. It was the first real problem I had experienced. It took three hours for me to get back to normal after the bad reaction to the blood.

We had received good news from Kent and Mark. They had called to tell us they were coming up the next day. I was anxious to see them again. I missed my boys and needed to see them and reassure myself that they were all right.

Friday January 31st, day 7.

I have never been very fond of eggs and will only eat them scrambled or cooked as hard as a brick with ketchup. I certainly have never wanted them with a runny yolk. For breakfast they had brought me a poached egg and toast, which I gladly ate. I remembered eating a poached egg one other time after one of the boys was born and was glad to get it then too. However, I did not want another one any time soon. When Helen Jo came in she took care of finding a menu for the upcoming meals so I could choose what I wanted. My appetite was not good but I was feeling hungry now.

One of the volunteers at the hospital, Mrs. Eleanor Letts, was wonderful to my family. On her first visit she brought the newspaper clippings about our accident and a 40-pound fruit basket! I don't remember if my family worked their way through the basket of fruit or not, but they certainly tried. Mrs. Letts told us on one of her visits that she was trying to get the local newspaper to do a "human interest" story on me and my family. My family had expressed to her how impressed they were with the hospital staff for the wonderful care given me, as well as the compassion and love shown by the people of the city who had stopped by to offer help. She also took Mom and Helen Jo to lunch one day.

I was receiving a few cards now that word was getting out about the accident and my injuries. On his daily radio program, our disc jockey friend, Dean Stevenson, had been giving daily updates on my condition and advising his listening audience specifically what to pray for each day. He was also giving my address at the hospital. There were other Gospel radio stations doing the same. Twenty cards and two packages arrived on this Friday. One of the packages contained a beautiful pink gown from my Aunt Bunny. The little note she had written on the bottom of the card made me cry a little but I loved what she had written as well as the gift. I had also received floral arrangements and potted plants but they could not be brought into ICU. I would have to wait until I was in a room of my own to enjoy them. One pretty little potted plant was from our good friends, Shirley Quick and Carole Cooper, who attended every one of our concerts they could get to. The nurse let Helen Jo bring it in and show it to me. I jokingly commented, "Oh, how pretty, I wonder how long it will take me to kill it!" I was well known for having a "brown thumb" where plants were concerned. Everyone laughed as I had hoped they would. And no, I did not kill it. Not right away.

One of the nurses had told me to start moving my right foot, work the ankle as much as I could. I did move it up and down even though it was quite painful. I don't know how much movement I was getting but they were very pleased with it and stressed how important it was that I keep it as limber as I could.

I was to have a bandage change that day and 30 minutes before the doctor and his assistant arrived, I was given a pain shot. Dick arrived first. I had learned right away that he was really the one who did the "dirty work" of removing the bandages. He was very gentle and used saline solution on the places where the bandages were stuck. He tried very hard not to cause me any more pain than he had to. Mom and Daddy and Kenny had gone to eat their dinner but Helen Jo had stayed with me because she did not want to miss seeing my legs. She asked Dick if he wanted her to leave and he said, "No, you said you wanted to see them." She assured him that she did and then she moved to stand beside me so she could hold my hand. She was much more excited about the bandage change than I was!

After the bandages were off Dr. Lancourt arrived to check my legs. He showed Helen Jo everything he had done and told her how good everything looked. He said there was one little place on my left leg that needed to be trimmed up, the tissue was dying, but that was no problem. He explained that he had used my heel pad to cushion the stump of the left leg. He said, "It's the best made . . . nature can't be duplicated in that area." (Nature to him, but God's creation to me. And yes it is the best made!) He went on to say that the right leg was clean and pink and healing well. In his words, "Clean is clean, not much to say about it." I had no temperature, and the circulation was good. He told us a plastic surgeon would be looking at my legs and then begin to do a little skin grafting, it probably would not be anything major. He said they were just so pleased with the way everything looked. He kept looking at Helen Jo to see if she was as pleased with the way my legs looked as they were, and of course, she was. She kept telling him how great my legs looked and that I was a miracle. The last time she had seen my legs was in the ER and I'm sure what she was seeing now was so much better. This was my first time to see them and all I could think of was that they looked like huge ham hocks! It was almost like I was looking at something that was not attached to me. I was not happy with what I saw but I was thankful I still had as much of my legs as I did. I tried to smile and have a happy face for everyone else. I did not tell anyone how I really felt.

Kenny, Mom and Daddy had made it back in time to see my legs then they all gathered around Dr. Lancourt and talked with him. Mom and Helen Jo gave him his hugs, which he always seemed ready for. Helen Jo also told him she would be going home for a few days but she planned to come back. However, just in case she did not get back she wanted him to know something. She asked him, "Do you remember in the ER when you told me you couldn't be my hero? Well, I'll tell you this, Jesus is the hero, you're the instrument." He said, "Well, that's okay."

Kent and Mark arrived around 9:00 PM and I was so glad to see them again. We had talked a lot about the accident all day off and on. After the boys arrival the conversation eventually turned in that direction again. It was interesting to get everyone's account of what they remembered about the accident and their feelings. Each of us had details that no one else had.

Kenny had made arrangements with Dick and Dixie Crump for Kent and Mark to stay in their home and after our visit the boys left and gladly accepted the Crump's hospitality. Being in a home was a much better atmosphere than the hospital and they really enjoyed staying with them. They had children about their age and a game room. Helen Jo sat with me until midnight and then daddy took the night shift.

Saturday February 1st, day 8.

I was going to be moved to 3E today but before they moved me Mary Schmitt, the nurse who had brushed the glass out of my hair came in to wash my hair and give me a bed bath. It was not an easy job but she did it very well and, oh, did it ever feel good to be clean from head to knees again. When she had finished, Helen Jo dried my hair with the blow dryer and then curled it a bit with a curling iron. I almost felt like a new woman but I was exhausted when it was all done. Everyone marveled at how good I looked and how far I had come in a week. It was nothing short of amazing.

Mary Schmitt escorted me up to 3E where the day nurse had stayed late on her shift to meet me and get me settled. I now had a semi-private room they had made private at Dr. Lancourt's request. He did not want another patient in the room with me because of my open wounds; there would be too much risk of infection. It was wonderful to be in a room all to myself and have my family all around me. I could also have the floral arrangements and plants, which had arrived during the first week as well as the new ones coming in. When Dr. Lancourt came to my room the first time and saw all of the flowers he asked my family who I was and if I was a celebrity. We all got a good laugh out of that! To this day it makes me grin to think about it.

While I was being settled in my new room, Kenny, Helen Jo, Kent and Mark had gone to the bus to take pictures. Helen Jo told me she crawled inside and found an unbelievable sight. There was so much more destruction than she had remembered, especially where I had been sitting. She was surprised and shocked at the amount of blood in the stairwell and soaking the blanket I had used to cover my feet and legs. She realized anew what a miracle I really was. I came to the same realization after they had the film developed and I saw the pictures of the bus.

Before I left the ICU, Barbara Tunks, one of my wonderful nurses, told Helen Jo that I would never know how many lives I had touched. She also said that she had been very *down* when I came into ICU. When she began taking care of me, it had lifted her spirits. When Helen Jo told me what she had said, I told her I didn't know how I had done that. She said she guessed it was because I suffered so quietly and still held on to Jesus and praised Him. I do have a great deal of faith in God and though I certainly do not understand why we had the accident and I was so badly injured, I do not believe God *made* it happen, but I do believe He *allowed* it to happen. One of my favorite songs, THROUGH IT ALL, kept going through my mind when I was in ICU hurting so badly and wondering, "Why." One line of the song is, "But in every situation God gave blessed consolation that my trials come only to make me strong." I think it did that.

Greg, Brad and Carolyn arrived and I was so glad to see them. I especially wanted to hear how Greg's legs were doing. He had gone to the doctor at home and they told him basically the same thing as the doctor at the hospital in St. Joseph. His knees and legs were badly bruised and it would take some time for them to heal. Once again we talked about the accident and each person voiced his or her feelings and fears throughout the whole ordeal. It was good to be able to talk with each other about it. The Moore's spent the night in St. Joe and returned home to Dexter, Missouri the next day. It had been good to see them and be with them for a little while.

Helen Jo was also going home on Sunday as Kent and Mark returned to Olive Branch. I hated to see them all go but I knew they had things to attend to. Helen Jo had received a call from Steve who was very sick with the first stages of pneumonia. He had been to the doctor and gotten medication but needed help with Matt. She would be going home to see about them. She had not seen Matt in nine days and was missing him a lot. And besides that, with his daddy so sick he was probably more certain than ever that he was going to starve to death if his mother did not come home.

Sunday February 2nd, day 9.

It was a quiet day after everyone left to go home. I do not remember if I cried when they left. If I was not crying on the outside I am sure I was on the inside. I just had this feeling of needing all of my people around me. I was so thankful Kenny and Mom and Daddy were still there. I was not ready to be alone. In fact, it would be a long time before I was comfortable being alone. Being confined to my bed and totally dependent on others was not a feeling I liked very well. Knowing I could not get up and walk any time I wanted or even get into a wheel chair on my own, left me feeling very vulnerable. I would not lose that feeling for many, many weeks.

Kent and Mark had brought me a Walkman tape player and some of my favorite Gospel cassettes. When I tried to listen to one of them it made me cry. It was quite unexpected because I love Gospel music. I found in the coming weeks that for some reason, Gospel music made me weepy. I could not listen to it. Perhaps deep down in my heart I thought I would never be able to go on stage and sing again. After all, at that point I was not even certain I would be able to stand again.

When Kent, Mark and Helen Jo arrived in Olive Branch they called to let us know they were safely home. It worried me that my family had to travel back and forth to St. Joseph. And, I missed them when they were gone. It was such a long trip and I was naturally concerned about them on the highway. I was beginning to wonder about my recovery and how long I would have to be in St. Joseph.

Monday February 3rd, day 10.

I got a surprise that morning when one of the nurses came in with a wheel chair and said I could sit up in it for a while. It took some doing to get me out of bed and into the chair but with the help of my trapeze bar, which Dr. Lancourt had ordered installed over the bed, I pulled myself up and the nurses got me to the edge of the bed and in the chair. After 45 minutes I was worn out. They told me I could sit up in it again that afternoon. Frankly I did not care if I did or not. I have to admit I was a bit scared at first. I think I just felt safer and more secure in the bed.

I received 6 more beautiful bouquets of flowers and one single rose from our dear friend, Elisha, in Georgia. I also got several cards, many with checks or cash tucked inside. Our relatives at home as well as friends all over the country were so loving and generous. It seemed everybody just wanted to do something to help.

Surgery was scheduled for the next morning. That afternoon I had an EKG as well as a visit from the anesthesiologist. Now that I was not being kept as sedated and was mentally alert enough to think about the surgery, I dreaded it. I was not too keen on being put to sleep again. This would be my third surgery.

Tuesday, February 4, day 11.

I was taken to surgery at 10:00 AM for more debridement and possible plastic surgery. I was out of surgery at 12:00 PM and awoke with a horrible headache. It felt like a migraine or bad sinus headache. The nurse thought it was probably from the anesthetic. Nothing helped it until Mom started applying hot moist towels to my forehead and had me use nose spray as the nurse suggested. It was one of the worst headaches I have ever had and it hung on the rest of the day. The surgery was successful and uneventful. Dr. Lancourt said he was able to correct the open wounds with the muscle and skin available. A plastic surgeon was not needed this time. One might be needed later on. Again, wait and see. I rested pretty well that night although there was more pain than usual because of the surgery and debridment. I was also still dealing with the headache. Daddy stayed the night with me again. I don't think they could have run him out with a stick. I know he could not have rested sitting in a chair but I would wake up and hear him praying for me and that was a comfort.

Wednesday, February 5th, day 12.

I awoke with the headache from the day before still hanging on but as the day went on it began to ease and leave. I was noticing a hoarseness after the surgeries and that bothered me. It never seemed to completely leave.

41

Dr. Lancourt had come in to check on me and he okayed the use of my allergy medication, which seemed to help the headache. He also said he wanted me to start eating more, especially lots and lots of ice cream. The hospital food was so unappealing I had not been able to eat much of anything. Turned out the poached egg and toast had been the best thing they had to offer. Before he left he told us that I would be taken back to surgery on Friday for more debridment and repair.

For a couple of days we had been talking about getting me home . . . at least to a hospital in Cape Girardeau, Missouri which would be within 30 minutes of my home. Although I did not want to leave my good doctor in St. Joe, I was getting homesick and did not like the fact that my family had to travel the long distance to see me. Transportation for me to southeast Missouri was discussed as well as what doctor to contact in Cape Girardeau. The travel options were: ambulance, helicopter or small plane. From the first Dr. Lancourt did not like the idea of a helicopter because of the vibration. He said it would be too hard on my legs and me. He was going to check on an ambulance.

Helen Jo had called to tell us she would be coming back to St. Joe on Friday. She had also gotten the name of an orthopedic surgeon. Our cousin, Carolyn, who was an RN at St. Francis Medical Center in Cape Girardeau, had suggested Dr. Michael Trueblood. She said that she had worked with him and in her opinion he was the best. Especially with accident injuries such as mine.

Dr. Lancourt had mentioned that he had a doctor friend at Carbondale, Illinois. He was a professor at the university. Since Carbondale was an hour from our home in Olive Branch, we only briefly considered it as an option. We told Dr. Lancourt that we did not know anything about that hospital and were much more familiar with both hospitals in Cape Girardeau and we knew they were both good. Dr. Lancourt said, "That's okay, the fancy professor probably wouldn't see her anyway, just some of his students." Then he went on to say, "I don't want her to be a guinea pig for anyone and I don't want her in a shitty hospital!" Then they told him that we had the name of a good orthopedic surgeon in Cape, one recommended by our cousin who was an RN and had worked with him many times. He said, "That's good. If a family member recommended the doctor in Cape he's probably okay." He was given the name and he said he would call Dr. Trueblood and talk with him. He would tell him about my case and find out how he felt about taking me as his patient. We agreed with that.

Thursday, February 6th, day 13.

It was a fairly quiet day. My family had several visitors. The lady in the red coat, Alice, was by the day before and sat with them while I was in recovery. Today a lady named Helga came and visited with them and brought me a book. Mr. Black was back in also. Dr. Lancourt made his routine visit and said everything looked good. They told me it was snowing and opened the drapes so I could see it. I had received thirty cards. Surgery was scheduled for the next day.

Friday, February 7th, day 14.

This was surgery number four. I was in a lot of pain when they brought me back to my room. Dr. Lancourt said I would not have to go back again soon. Thank God for that! I had not woken up with a headache this time but the hoarseness in my throat was worse than ever. I mentioned it to my nurse and she told me it was from the tube they put down my throat during the surgeries. She suggested I tell the anesthesiologist before the next surgery and to be sure and tell him I am a singer.

Kent, Helen Jo and Steve left Olive Branch at 9:00 that morning on their way to St. Joe. Steve's parents had come to stay with Matt. Mom and Daddy were planning to go home on Sunday morning. After the bandage change, which was scheduled for Monday, we were all hoping we would know more about transferring me to a hospital in Cape Girardeau.

Kent, Helen Jo and Steve arrived in St. Joe around 6:30. I was glad to see them again. They had brought all of my mail from home and I looked at my cards as we visited and caught up on what was going on at home. I was glad to see that Steve was well and to hear that Matt had not starved to death as he thought he would. After that Kenny filled them in on the outcome of the surgery that morning. The doctor had done a lot of work on my legs and right half-foot and I had been in a lot of pain all day. He told Kenny and my parents that they still might have to take four or five inches off the left leg. It was not healing as fast as the right one and he did not think that was a good sign. I had a bad night with a lot of pain that night. The debridement must have been very extensive. Every nerve ending was crawling and burning and the phantom pains were terrible.

Saturday, February 8th, day 15.

Because of the pain medication, and perhaps the pain itself, I was hot all the time, especially my face. The only thing to give me relief from it was to continuously wipe my face with a cold wet cloth. That made it impossible to wear make-up. Besides not really feeling like applying it anyway, I knew it would be a waste of time and good make-up to apply it every day just to wipe it off a few minutes later with the wet cloth. For someone who had never gone out of the house without my "face" on, that was a very big change.

Kenny sat with me Saturday night so Daddy could get a good night's sleep before driving home on Sunday. He had insisted on sitting with me every night since they had been there and he was exhausted.

Today was Kenny's 49th birthday.

Sunday, February 9th, day 16.

Mom and Daddy left after breakfast heading home. Kent was staying on until Monday. Again my family was on the road and that worried me. I would learn later on that traveling on the road would not only worry me for my loved ones but I would be very uncomfortable traveling the highways for years to come. I am especially uncomfortable on the interstate highways with 18-wheelers all around me driving at high speeds.

I had found out that being in my own room had brought about many changes and certain advantages. My family could now bring in food. Wonderful, glorious fast food! The hospital food was terrible and I could not eat it. Their kitchen was under renovation and the food was being catered in. One thing about it, it was consistently tasteless and the same awful color of gray! The staff knew how awful the food was and encouraged my family to bring in anything I thought I might be able to eat. They brought in KFC, pizza, burgers and fries, etc. and I began to eat a little better. However, eating better had brought on another problem. I could not use that horrible bedpan. I told the nurse that I was sure I could use the commode if I could get into the bathroom. However, it was impossible to get the wheel chair in the bathroom and then get me out of it and on the commode. And, because of the pins sticking up out of my legs, it was too risky. I was miserable.

Around 7:45 Sunday night Jeff Potts and a friend, Dana, arrived. Jeff had played guitar and sung with our group for a couple of years. He had heard about our accident but could not find out much about it. He decided to drive from Springfield, Missouri to St. Joseph to find out for himself how I was. When he walked in I broke down and cried. I could not believe he would drive all that distance that day to see me and then turn around and drive back after visiting for a couple of hours. It was a good visit though I still tired very easily and still had the bedpan problem.

Around 10:00 that night after Jeff and Dana had left, Kathy, one of my night nurses, solved my bathroom problem when she hit on the idea of bringing in a shower chair. There are two great things about a shower chair. One, it's on wheels and two, it has a seat with no bottom in the very center. She came wheeling the chair through my door with this look of triumph on her pretty face, grinning from ear to ear. To be certain her calculations were correct she took it on in the bathroom and rolled it over the commode. A perfect fit! She was confident she and a couple of other nurses could get me out of bed and on the chair, wheel me into the bathroom, position the chair over the pot and let nature take it's course. The biggest problem was getting me out of bed with the pins sticking up out of my legs. They had a tendency to lock together if I let one leg get too close to the other. When the time came for the trial run on the shower chair, I pulled myself up with the trapeze bar and the nurse moved my legs around and got me to the edge of the bed. Two of them lifted me onto the chair while the other held my legs and kept the pins from getting tangled, and away we went! After they had the chair over the commode they propped my legs on a pillow on a chair and excused themselves to wait in the other room. It had taken three strong young women to accomplish the deed but they were as thrilled as I was when we got the job done. Literally!

Helen Jo stayed with me Sunday night to give Kenny a chance for a good nights sleep. I don't recall ever asking anyone to stay with me at night but somehow they knew I needed them there and someone always was.

Monday, February 10th, day 17.

Around 6:00 AM Kenny came in to sit with me while Helen Jo went to clean up and get breakfast. While she was gone I had a bed bath and changed gowns. My hair had been washed and curled on Sunday and looked better this time than the time before. I had been due a trim when we had the accident so it was too long and harder to handle. Helen Jo said I looked pretty and was looking better. I did not feel it but it's always nice to get a compliment. I did not seem to be as hot all the time and was not doing as much face wiping with the wet cloth. That was a definite improvement.

I had been told earlier when the nurse was in that they would be changing bandages that day and, as usual, I dreaded it. It was always painful and got the nerve endings all stirred up afresh and it would take all day to get them settled back down to a tolerable level.

Not long after Helen Jo relieved Kenny the nurses came in with the wheel chair, got me out of bed and into it and Helen Jo took me on a tour of the hospital. She showed me both bridges, which were waiting or lounge areas. She also took me to the chapel and then showed me the Stay Inns where they were staying and how close it was to ICU where I had been the first eight days. When we got back to the room the nurse said that Dr. Lancourt and Dick were there to do the bandage change. The pain medication from earlier in the day had worn off and the doctor had not called ahead for a pain shot. They were going to try to do this bandage change without the pain shot. I was not thrilled to hear that because the bandage changes were painful with the pain medication. I had an idea it was not going to be a party without the pain shot! The elastic bandages were not a problem but the gauze was stuck tight and when Dick started trying to get it loose it was so painful I began to cry. Dick sent someone for saline solution to soak the gauze and help loosen it but it was still horribly painful. Helen Jo was holding my hand and praying and trying to talk me through it. Barbara, my nurse, asked me if I wanted my pain pills. I told her no. By the time they took effect it would all be over. Helen Jo got me a cold wet cloth and bathed my face. Dr. Lancourt called a halt to the unwrapping and ordered a pain shot. They gave the shot 5 minutes to work and then started again. Barbara, my nurse was having me take deep breaths to help control the pain. Finally, Dick had both legs unwrapped. My whole body was as tense as it had been in ICU several days before.

Dr. Lancourt began explaining to everyone how everything was looking and how far the healing had come. He said the open gash on the front of my right leg (on the shin bone and along side of it) had been pulled together as much as it could be and stitched. The muscle had been pulled around to cover the bone. Instead of a twelve-inch open wound I now had about a four-inch open wound, which would need plastic surgery in the near future. The gash around the back of my calf, almost in the bend of my leg, the one he had said initially that he could put his hand down in, was stitched and was beginning to heal nicely. He had done some shaping work on the stump of my right foot so that when I started to walk I would not be clumsy. He said that leg and foot were looking very good. This was the leg he had told us would have to come off above the knee that morning in the ER. He said he was amazed at how it was healing. He said my left leg was healing much more slowly. The stump had been trimmed as much as possible now without taking off four or five more inches. After the doctor and Dick left I told Helen Jo that I did not want to have to go through that and she said she did not believe I would have to. We were still believing for a miracle.

I don't remember if Kenny and Kent had been in my room for the bandage change or if they were outside in the hall. If they had been in the room, I think they left when the pain got so bad that I was crying and yelling. They both said they just wanted to hit something or somebody. It must have been awful to watch and hear.

After the pain shot really kicked in Helen Jo left to meet Steve for dinner. While they were out Kenny and Kent stayed with me. As usual, after Helen Jo had eaten she went to her room to rest a while and answer or make calls. She had returned to my room and Kenny and Kent had left for their dinner, when the nurse came in to hook me up for another blood transfusion. This one went better than the last one had but as a precaution they took my temperature every 30 minutes. They wanted to make sure there was no bad reaction to this one. After I was successfully transfused with the additional unit of blood, it brought the total to twelve units all together. Thank God I had not had another bad reaction. I know Helen Jo, as well as others, had really prayed about the blood transfusion.

Tuesday, February 11th, day 17.

I woke up with another headache and again had trouble getting over it, although it was not as bad as the other had been. I still did not have much of an appetite and was not eating as well as the doctor wanted me to. Helen Jo was sitting with me and I had fallen asleep when a loud knock on the door woke me. It was Dr. Lancourt and Dick. I was surprised to see them because it was not time to change bandages and I was a bit apprehensive about why they were there. He had just stopped by on his rounds to check on my blood count and me since the transfusion. He told us that my blood counts were fine and everything was looking good. He had not called Dr. Trueblood yet, but would soon. Then we would know when I could go home. He said they would change my bandages the next morning but he had already ordered a big pain shot for fifteen minutes before their arrival. He was very upbeat and encouraging and had started calling Helen Jo his "girlfriend." They had developed a good rapport since the morning in the ER seventeen days earlier. I think he had come to appreciate her spunk. I doubt he had ever had anyone tell him that he could not do something.

The Chaplin the hospital had assigned to my case chose this day to "counsel" Helen Jo about giving me false hopes and me about accepting my situation. I did not understand his thinking at all. His faith certainly was no match for ours. In truth he was quite negative. He told me several times to read the book of Job in the Bible. I told him that I had read Job and didn't like it the first time I read it and didn't intend to read it again . . . at least not any time soon. I know he meant well but he was not helping us spiritually. After his counseling Helen Jo called our pastor, James Drysdale, and received encouraging and uplifting counseling which made both of us feel better.

Kenny and Kent went out and got us a bucket of KFC for our dinner that night and right after we had eaten Dr. Lancourt called. He had talked with Dr. Trueblood and was very impressed with the doctor and the medical center. He said Dr. Trueblood had answered all of his questions satisfactorily and he felt very good about sending me to Cape Girardeau. The next day we would talk about the transfer and how it would be done.

Wednesday, February 12th, day 18.

Helen Jo stayed with me Tuesday night to give Kenny a rest. I had a more restful night. The pain had not been as constant unless the pain medication was wearing off. Around 7:00 Kenny came and sat with me and Helen Jo went to clean up and eat breakfast. When she came back later my mail had come and we were looking at the cards when in popped Dr. Lancourt. Again I was apprehensive seeing him when it was not time for him to be there. I immediately told him not to touch my legs and I reminded him that he said I could have a pain shot before bandage changes. He assured me that I would get the shot before bandages were changed. He had come in early to give us the information about transportation to Cape Girardeau. He had found out that it would cost $2,000 to transfer me via ambulance. A helicopter would be almost as much but was not an option as far as he was concerned. He did not know about the price of a small plane. He asked Kenny to check with our insurance to see what we wanted to do. Kenny went off to call the insurance company and the doctor left to send the nurse in with the pain shot. In ten minutes Dick and Dr. Lancourt came in for the bandage change. The change went much better than the one on Monday. It was still very painful but not nearly as bad. Dr. Lancourt seemed very proud of his work and so pleased with the healing. He said, "The right leg is coming right along. The left leg is pinking up and is tender. I expect it to heal." Very good news! Up until then he had always said that four or five more inches might still have to come off the left leg. Another miracle. Then he surprised us by saying, "Whatever you're doing, keep doing it. It's working." I'm sure he knew by now that we were praying, Bible-believing people. It was for sure he knew we were Christians because Helen Jo had told him that up front. Before he left he said the nurse would be teaching me how to take care of the area around the pins so they would not get infected. When Dick rebandaged my legs, after cleaning around the pins, he used less gauze than ever before. We all discussed the arrangements for transfer and Dick helped me decide on how I wanted to go. He really recommended an airplane because it would be less tiring and a smoother ride. He said the 9-hour ambulance ride would be very tiring and could be rough. A helicopter would definitely be the least desirable. The vibration would not be good for my legs. After the decision was made for transfer via small plane Kenny and Dr. Lancourt put together the final plans. Social Services would come in the next day to help finalize everything.

It usually took the rest of the day, if not longer, to recoup from the dressing changes. My appetite still was not good but when Kenny and Kent suggested pizza it sounded good and that was what we had for dinner that night. I ate 2 slices and a cup of peaches from my hospital dinner tray. The most I had eaten since before the accident. We had visitors as we usually did every night. They prayed for us and ministered to us. After visiting hours Kenny, Helen Jo and I finished the cold pizza then settled down for the night.

Thursday, February 13th, day 19.

Helen Jo had been collecting the RN's and LPN's names and addresses, as well as the visitors over the last couple of days in preparation for my transfer. There had been a lot of hugging and well wishes, etc. Everyone wanted to be kept advised as to my progress when I arrived at St. Francis in Cape. On this particular day she had gone to ICU to see those ladies but had only caught two of the ones who had taken care of me. Back in her room she answered a knock on her door and it was Traci Boyer and Shirley Lutz from the first morning in ER. When she got back to my room Cheryl from ER and Chris from REHAB were just going in. I had questions for Chris about prosthetics, what I might expect, etc. After they left I was a bit depressed over the answers I had gotten to my questions. I could see I was going to have a lot of adjusting to do. Helen Jo and I talked about it and I cried. It was not the first tears I had shed about my loss nor would they be the last. I also shared with Helen Jo that it was very difficult to handle the feeling that my right half-foot was bound and the toes turned under. Of course, it was wrapped, both with gauze bandage as well as elastic bandage. The elastic wrapping was supposed to help desensitize my "stumps." (I may as well say here just how I feel about that ugly word "stump." I have disliked it from the beginning and continue to feel the same about it today. I seldom use it to refer to my legs and feet and only use it now because it is, after all, the medical term to describe them.) After Helen Jo and I had talked for a good while about some of the feelings I had been having I felt better. We both agreed that God was still in control and He was going to take care of the little things just as He had the big ones.

After our talk I took my "bird bath," put make-up on and fixed my hair. That pretty well wore me out and I was resting when Barbara Tunks, my first nurse in ICU, came in with a little going away gift for me, something to remember her by. It was a pretty little glass collector Blue Bird of Happiness. I still have it and remember her when I look at it. Our dear friend Dixie, who had been our laundress and host to the boys when they were in town, also came to say goodbye. Dr. Lancourt and Dick were the next to arrive. We now had a room full. After Dixie left Dr. Lancourt and Dick checked my legs and were visibly pleased at the progress I had made. Dick was grinning from ear to ear. Kenny took pictures of them and then Helen Jo showed them the pictures of the wrecked bus. Dr. Lancourt told me that he felt certain I would be back at my career in time. Because of what he had been able to do for me, he knew I had great potential ahead. He said it had been nice meeting me but he was sorry about the circumstances. He promised he would try to remember to send a copy of the pictures he had taken in the OR that first morning. He also said he wanted pictures of me when I was up and walking, as well as progress letters from time to time. As we shook hands I told Dr. Lancourt and Dick that I loved and appreciated them and all they had done for me and I would always have a special place in my heart for them. Then Dr. Lancourt turned to Helen Jo, held his arms out and said, "Well, gal . . . ?" She said, "I guess you want your hugs?" She hugged him and Dick as she had done many times in the past several days. The day before, she had given both of them our latest cassette, "Of A Special Kind." Dick told her he had listened to it the night before and he liked it. Dr. Lancourt asked him how the Mormons felt about that. After that remark we assumed that Dick was of the Mormon faith. After Dr. Lancourt and Dick left Barbara said her goodbye. She also told us how much I had meant to her, explaining that she had been so "burned out" career-wise, that she had planned to quit the following Monday after I arrived in the ICU that Saturday morning. Taking care of me had turned that around for her and we would never know how much I had meant to her. I was very humbled by that but I knew it was not me she was seeing but Jesus in me. He was my strength when I had none of my own. As I lay there in such pain I kept thinking of Jesus on the cross and how he must have suffered and I knew what I was dealing with was just a portion of the pain He had suffered. If He could take what He did, I could handle mine.

Hospital volunteer, Eleanor Letts, had been successful in arranging for the local newspaper to do a human-interest story about our group, the accident and me. Before Phyllis Wright, the reporter, began the interview she and the photographer asked Kenny, Kent, Steve and Helen Jo to walk outside with them for a couple of photos in front of the hospital. When they came back to my room we all took part in the hour and a half interview. Lori Goodson, a reporter for the hospital's paper, was also there for the interview. It was a good and positive experience and the article in the newspaper was factual and accurate. After the two reporters had left Eleanor, who had also been present for the interview, took Helen Jo out to eat.

The plan was for me to be flown out of St. Joseph the next day. Helen Jo spent the evening organizing things and packing up for our departure. She dismantled all of the fresh floral arrangements I had received and made 2 large bouquets. She took one to the nurse's station on the third floor and the other to the ICU nurses. After that she began trying to consolidate all of the things in my room for the trip home. She said she, "Couldn't find enough stuff to put all of the stuff in." Some of the stuff she was referring to included my gifts. Up to that time I had received 318 cards, 28 floral arrangements (fresh cut flowers as well as potted plants), 6 gowns, 1 bed jacket and 2 robes. By 10:30 that night she finally had things organized to her satisfaction and left for her room to get cleaned up. She would relieve Kenny later on so he could get a good night's rest before driving home the next day. Steve and Kent had gone to Dick and Dixie's to play pool for a while. Kenny stayed with me. He and Kent would be driving the cars back to southern Illinois with all of the "stuff" Helen Jo had organized. Steve, Helen Jo and I would be flying to Cape. By the time we got settled down around 1:00 AM I was hurting pretty badly. I had not gotten my pain pills on time and the pain was a bit out of control by the time they came. It took a while to get my legs settled down again.

Friday, February 14th, day 20.

The hospital must have been very busy the night before because it was a noisy night on my floor and that was unusual. With the late arrival of my pain pills and the time it took for my legs to settle down plus the noise, it was difficult for us to rest. I'm sure I had a bit more sleep than Helen Jo because of the pain pills. Regardless, we were awake early and began getting dressed and ready for the long awaited transfer. When Helen Jo returned from getting dressed and ready to go she found me sitting up in bed and Kenny on the phone. From his end of the conversation it sounded like our flight was probably snowed out for today. We would try again the next day, hopefully around noon. Helen Jo went back to tell Steve and Kent the news and then called Mom and Dad to let them know. Ann from Social Services, who had been making all of the arrangements, was doing all of the legwork and would keep us updated. At noon she came in to tell us we were scheduled for 3:00 PM the next afternoon.

When Dr. Lancourt and Dick came to check my legs they noted the change of discharge on my chart, which meant that I would be there at least another day. The doctor said that as long as I was there he would take care of me. He also mentioned that there had been some murmurings about bandage changes and being short handed in Cape. They had asked if the bandages could be changed here before I left. Dr. Lancourt was not happy with the sound of that and was about ready to change his mind about Cape. He went on to say that he was not going to say goodbye again. He ordered pin care (cleaning around the Hoffman pins) even if they didn't get my bandages changed. He asked Helen Jo to call Dr. Trueblood's secretary in Cape and let her know the arrangements. She could not reach anybody in the office and finally called his home. He talked with her and told her that Social Services had reached him and he knew of the change. He also told her that his partner would see me over the weekend and he would start all over with me on Monday. Although Helen Jo did not voice it at the time, she was beginning to wonder if the move was the right thing. In my mind I was wondering the same thing. I was torn between leaving Dr. Lancourt and Dick who had taken such good care of me and who we had come to love so much, and starting all over with a doctor we knew nothing about, except that he was a good doctor. However, for me, there was always the pull of home.

Saturday, February 15th, day 21.

Again Helen Jo stayed the night with me so Kenny could rest up for the drive home. We slept better than the night before and were awake by 7:00 or 7:30. Helen Jo went to get dressed and eat breakfast. When she came back to my room she washed my hair, dried and curled it then I bathed and dressed in a clean gown and warm robe. For the second or third day

I decided to apply make up even though the cold wet washcloth was still in use. I continued to perspire from the pain medication but I wanted to look my best for the flight to Cape.

Kenny called Mr. Taylor in Carbondale for confirmation that the plane would be flying out as planned. He said everything was "go" on the Carbondale end. Social Services confirmed that all was go on the Heartland end. Around 11:00 the guys started carrying everything out and loading it in the cars for transporting home to Olive Branch.

Dr. Lancourt and Dick arrived to change my bandages and said everything looked good. Helen Jo was glad to get one more look at my legs because she did not know if she would get to see them at St. Francis in Cape or not. Once again, Dr. Lancourt said that he wasn't going to say goodbye again. I think he was having second thoughts about letting me go and was only doing it because it was what I needed emotionally. He told us he would really like to see this through because he liked to finish what he started. After Dick had my legs rebandaged he showed us pictures of his kids. I wish we could have just loaded Dr. Lancourt and Dick up and taken them with us. The parting with these two wonderful men was turning out to be much more difficult than I had imagined it would be. We had come to love them very much in the twenty days we had been at Heartland West.

Kenny and Kent left for home at noon. They would see us in Cape the next morning. Their trip south would take much longer than ours. Oh, how I hated to see them make that long drive but it would be the last time it was necessary.

The time passed slowly for Helen Jo and me and Steve between noon and the time the ambulance was to pick us up and drive us to the airport. The sweet little man in overalls came over to say goodbye. I could tell he was surprised to see me looking so good with my hair freshly done and make up on. He said he was so happy for me that I was getting to transfer closer to my home and he wished me the very best.

The EMT's were a little late picking us up and getting us to the airport but we arrived just as the plane from Carbondale was landing. After the plane had refueled they got me loaded as quickly and easily as possible. The plane was an eight or ten passenger. They had taken enough of the seats out on the right side of the plane so a stretcher could be placed on the floor and bolted down for the flight. I had a wonderful view of the ceiling of the plane for the entire trip. It was Helen Jo and Steve's first flight and they were excited about that. The pilot told Steve he could sit in the right seat beside him and Steve was as tickled as a kid in a candy store. Helen Jo was seated behind me on the left side, I believe. The flight took two hours and though I have never been a comfortable flier, it was much better than a nine-hour ambulance ride. When we landed at the Cape Girardeau Airport an ambulance was there waiting. So were Daddy and Mom. The only hitch in the transfer was that the EMT's in St. Joseph had not given us my records. They forgot and so did we. I had thought to ask Helen Jo about them when we were forty minutes into the flight which was a little too late. We had to have them wired to St. Francis.

When the EMT's at Cape unloaded me from the plane into the ambulance they had me totally wrapped up with blankets with nothing but my nose sticking out. Even though Cape Girardeau is eight hours farther south, it was much colder in Cape than it had been when we left St. Joseph. When we arrived at St. Francis, Helen Jo took care of the paper work while I was taken to a room with Mom and Dad following along. It was a semi-private room, which already had a woman with a broken leg in one of the beds. I requested a private room but they said they did not have one available. I insisted, as did Helen Jo, and after a conference with their supervisor they moved me to another semi-private room alone and they said they would keep it that way as long as they could. Someone could stay with me at night unless another patient had to be moved in and then it would be a problem. I was on the list for a private room. After the paper work was all done and the confusion over a private room settled, Mom and Daddy went on home and Helen Jo stayed the night with me. The aides brought in an old recliner for Helen Jo to sleep in. I was hoping she could rest well because I knew she must be worn out and near exhaustion. They would not give me the same pain medication, Percidan, I had been given at Heartland. I was given three Tylenol and that would have to do. I suppose that was because they did not have my records as yet.

So far my experience with the new hospital had not been especially good. Once again I was hoping I had made the right decision in deciding to transfer. At this time it did not look promising. Taking into consideration that my arrival had been on a weekend that was probably a factor. I would wait and see what another day would bring.

**The Galatians Quartet Publicity Photograph prior to the accident.
Steve, Helen Jo, Greg and Deanna**

**The Galatians Quartet Band Publicity Photograph prior to the accident.
Brad, Mark and Kent**

Deanna and Helen Jo with Wendy Bagwell in September 1985. The Galatians opened for Wendy's band, Wendy Bagwell and the Sunliters, on several occasions.

Deanna and Helen Jo with Kenny Hinson in January 1986. The Galatians opened for The Hinson's on several occasions. This was the last concert in which The Galatians performed before the accident.

Front view of the bus after the accident.

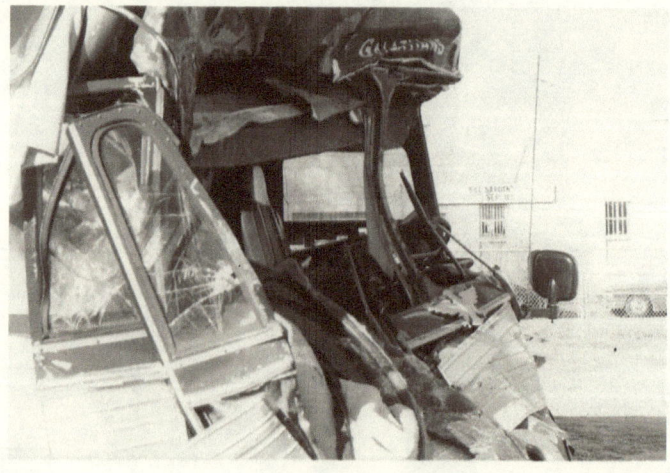

Side view of the bus after the accident.

Deanna and Rev. Dean Stevenson. This photo was taken at Dea's first public appearance after the accident at Marion Civic Center on February 1986; one month after the accident.

Deanna and Helen Jo's son, Matt. This was taken on one of Deanna's weekend passes home from the hospital; March 2, 1986. Prior to skin grafting. Pins were still in her legs before the casts were put on.

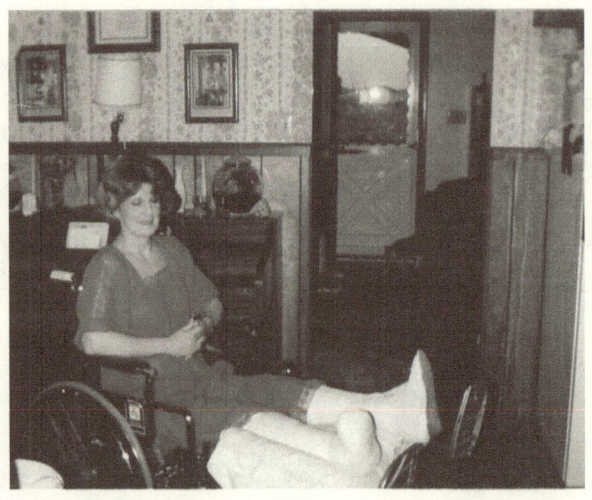

Deanna at home on weekend pass from the hospital; March 1986.
Pins have been removed and casts are now on both legs.

Deanna's first concert after the accident. Concert was held at the
Southern Illinois Quartet Convention on March 21, 1986. This was the
only concert in which Deanna sang from a wheel chair.

The Gospel CD of Deanna, her sister, Helen Jo and her daughter-in-law, Geinger that was recorded in 2009.

A recent photo of the family taken at Ken and Deanna's 50th wedding anniversary.

PART THREE

St. Francis Hospital—
Cape Girardeau, Missouri

February 16th.

We had slept fairly well and at 7:00 we found out that rising and shining was an hour earlier at St. Francis than at Heartland. Up at 7:00 and had my breakfast and bath by 8:30. Mom and Daddy arrived shortly after that.

At 9:15 Dr. Trueblood's partner arrived. I immediately did not like his "bedside manner." He promptly and rather abruptly removed my bandages. He looked at my legs and said, "The ideal amputee locations is 4 or 5 inches more off the left leg and the remaining part of the right foot should come off at the ankle." Helen Jo told him that we had heard that before but that Dr. Lancourt had been working to save as much as possible. The doctor asked her if he was an orthopedist and she told him yes. He then said, "He probably wasn't pushing for this since he wasn't going to be the optimum care giver. I'm just sure Dr. Trueblood will feel the same way, but the decision will be between you and him." After he left Helen Jo and I both just squalled! We were hurt and discouraged and very angry. Helen Jo said we were just going to have to teach these guys from the start just as we had the others. Mom, who had heard the whole thing kept telling me and Helen Jo that this doctor was not my doctor and not to get upset until we saw Dr. Trueblood the following morning. We got ourselves settled down and straightened up. Before bedtime I felt like I had the victory over the situation. I had decided it was time for me to take over responsibility for myself, decisions being made, etc. I had prayed a lot about it and was sure I was where I was supposed to be and I knew that if I had to I could, and would, make my own stand with my doctor the next morning. Of course, I would still welcome all the back up I could get from Kenny and Helen Jo should it be necessary. I was feeling much braver but not totally tough yet!

Mom had come prepared to stay the night with me Sunday night. After visiting for a while Daddy took Helen Jo home. She was in dire need of rest and lots of it. Matt was with them and was disturbed because his mommy was crying on the way home. She said she just couldn't stop. I think the whole ordeal had finally caught up with her and the doctor's visit had been the last straw. She had been so strong the whole 3 weeks but there comes a time when even the strongest need to rest and recoup. Her time had come.

Daddy took Matt home with him and Helen Jo went home and straight to bed. She slept until 3:30 that afternoon which was as long as Matt could stand it. He wanted to go home and be with his mommy. While Helen Jo had been sleeping, Daddy had told Kenny about the doctor's visit that morning and it made Kenny as angry as it had Helen Jo and me. When he got back home after visiting hours that night he talked with Helen Jo and told her that if things did not look different on Monday morning when we saw Dr. Trueblood that they would fly me back to St. Joe. She was in total agreement.

The day had not been a total loss. The first positive note of the day was a visit from Sister Jane Kiefer from pastoral care. She came into my room very quietly, as was her way, and we chatted for a bit and then she prayed for me. She would visit nearly every day the whole time I was hospitalized. We came to love her very dearly and we remain in touch with her.

The next positive was seeing Kenny, Kent and Mark walk in. Kenny and Kent told of their trip home with all of the plants and gifts. It had been long but uneventful. Then I found out that Mark had not felt well when everybody was in St. Joe and he was the only one at home for several days. When Mom and Dad had gotten back to Olive Branch they called to check on him and he was still not feeling up to par. Mom fed him a good supper and he felt much better right away. Then she found out that all he had been eating was fried Polish Sausage. Little wonder the kid was sick.

February 17th.

I had rested fairly well Sunday night although the Tylenol did not ease the pain like real pain medication. Helen Jo, Kenny and Kent were at the hospital early. They all wanted to be there when the doctor came. Unbeknownst to Helen Jo, and me Kenny and Kent had been waiting for the doctor's arrival and talked with him in the hall before he came into my room. Kenny told him how unhappy we had been with the doctor the day before and the manner in which he had handled things. Dr. Trueblood told him that things would change now. Kenny said, "If they don't change we have been told we can bring her back to St. Joe." Dr. Trueblood agreed. When Dr. Trueblood came in his manner was much better than the other doctor's had been. I found out right away that he had a very dry sense of humor and liked to kid around. That was fine with me. However, when he was talking about my wounds and treatment he was very serious. He unbandaged my legs and looked them over thoroughly. He thought everything looked very good but he did say that the right foot might have to come off above the ankle for a good prosthetic fit. He ordered physical therapy in a whirlpool two times a day. Oh, boy! I was in for another new experience, and it was to begin immediately, that day.

I had not liked the statement about my right foot but Helen Jo and I had already prayed about that in St. Joe and we continued to believe that additional amputation was not going to be necessary. I was not going to lose any more of my left leg or my right foot.

The first whirlpool treatment was very scary. Nobody had explained what was going to happen and I did not know what to expect. They lifted me on the stretcher, with a hoist, and then lowered me into the huge whirlpool. I don't know why that was so scary for me but it was! And then the shock of the water hitting the open wounds was very painful. Afterward the nerve endings were so stirred up they were burning and felt like so many bugs were crawling under the skin. It was always difficult to lie still when they were hurting like that but from previous surgeries and bandage changes I knew I had to. Moving around only made them hurt worse. About the time they had settled down from the morning session it was time to go back that afternoon.

The second session that afternoon was much the same. I was still scared when I was lifted into the tub and the water was just as painful. The aide, Freida, who helped with the process, was very sweet and compassionate as she tried to ease my distress. She said something nice to me about being a Christian too and told me she was praying for me. And, I started crying. At times I would cry at the drop of a hat anyway, not out of pity for myself, but because I was hurting and scared and it was crying time!

Another thing I had not been told was that the therapist would be doing debridement after I had been in the whirlpool that afternoon. Always before I had been in surgery and asleep when debridement was done. I had not been given any pain medication and I just had to grit my teeth and bear it. When it got too painful Barbara Wedekind, my physical therapist, would stop. I was thankful for that because it did get very painful at times.

During the afternoon session Dr. Trueblood walked in and saw me crying. He came over and asked me if it was hurting. I told him yes, but I was not crying about that, I was just weepy. He stood at the head of the stretcher and rubbed my neck and shoulder and kidded around with me as Barb finished up. After that little show of support and compassion from him I decided maybe he would be okay after all. I did like him, I just was not sure I trusted him yet. Later that evening he came into my room again to check on me. This was the third time he had seen me that day. I figured he probably wanted to be sure I was not sitting around crying all the time. I really was not, although I did have my moments. When the tears did come from time to time it would hit me like a wave and overwhelm me. If Kenny or some of my family were around they would just let me cry it out. Sometimes they would cry with me.

At some point during the day, Mom and Daddy had brought a Birthday Cake. It was my 45th birthday, Steve's 31st and my maternal Grandmother's 86th. The whole family was there, Kenny and the boys, Steve and Helen Jo and little Matthew. They had bent the rules a little and said that he could come in and eat cake with us. For a three year old he was really handling his Aunt Dea's injuries very well. Helen Jo, Steve, Kent and Mark had bought me a big purple bear named Zsa Zsa Gabear complete with boa around her shoulders and a flower behind her ear. I loved it and do to this day. Another gift to treasure as I do the blue bird from Barbara in St. Joe. I had also received flowers, balloons and many cards. All of the nurses wished me happy birthday and two of my therapist had sung Happy Birthday to me. I had many visitors and phone calls throughout the day. With the exception of the whirlpool sessions it had been a pretty good day.

February 18th.

It was my second day in the whirlpool followed by debridement by my therapist, Barb. I did not like it any better the second day than I had the first but I managed to get through it without crying. Barb was very sweet and compassionate and I liked her really well.

When Dr. Trueblood came to my room to check on me later, he told me I would be taken to surgery on Wednesday for better alignment of the bone in my left leg, more extensive debridement and skin grafting on the stump of my right foot as well as the wound on the shin of my right leg. There would also be skin grafting to the heel pad and stump on the left leg. I told him I did not know anything about skin grafts and asked him to explain how it was done. He said they would take a layer of skin off of my left thigh and lay a small section of the donor skin on the wound then bandage it and leave it undisturbed for 5 days. I asked him how successful skin grafts usually are. He said, "You know, when you plant zinnias sometimes they all come up, sometimes a few come up and sometimes none come up." That was how it worked with skin grafts. As he was leaving I thought to myself, okay, now we know we need to pray for a good crop, so to speak.

I really dreaded another surgery, but I did get a chance to tell the anesthesiologist about the hoarseness after the previous surgeries. He said he understood and would use a smaller tube. I told him I did not want to put myself in jeopardy because I did know how important it was to breath. He said it was no problem. Unfortunately I found out later on that the damage to my throat, or vocal cords, had already been done. I continue to have hoarseness in my throat, which sometimes affects my singing. I try to work around it as much as possible, but sometimes it is just there.

February 19th.

Surgery went as planned. Afterwards I was kept medicated for the pain and the day was very foggy for me. I remember having visitors but was too out-of-it to remember who they all were. A man and his wife from a nearby town had come by. She was an amputee and wanted to encourage me. It was nice of her to do that but I had only a vague memory of her being there.

The most painful part of the surgery was the donor site. It burned like fire all day and was very uncomfortable. As far as the other adjustments, they were painful but bearable. The bandages were thicker and tighter, probably to keep the grafts in place. I think the gauze bandages were wrapped with ace bandages. When they were removed Dr. Trueblood said he would know if the grafts had "taken."

The floor nurse came in to tell us that the doctor wanted my "night watchers" to cease. I wondered why he had not told us since he had just been in my room. Maybe it was time, but I was not ready. It is a very insecure feeling to know you cannot stand up and move around on your own. I would be thinking about it though.

When Helen Jo came she brought me a wonderful cup of coffee from Hardees, which I really enjoyed. It was my first cup since January 24th. I love coffee but had not been able to stomach the hospital coffee.

February 20th.

No more whirlpools! Thank God for that. Regular physical therapy, working out with weights and machines, began today. A walk in the park compared to the whirlpool.

Freida came to pick me up for the first physical therapy session. This was my first experience with the "transfer board." A slick board used to transfer from bed to chair and visa versa. I made the transfer into the wheel chair and she wheeled me to the physical therapy room. After Freida left me there Barbara showed me the things she wanted me to do which took about 30 minutes and wore me out. After she was sure I knew how to do everything she went on about her business of helping others. I really did not need her help with what I was doing. I had always had a lot of strength in my arms and legs and the exercises were not a problem for me. However, I did have a problem with the wheel chair, I had never wheeled one of them on my own and did not know how to go about it. I kept working with it until I learned how to go forward and backward and could negotiate it fairly well. At least I think I did. I never ran over anyone, but I did curb it a time or two.

February 21st.

I woke up excited today . . . my hair stylist of many years, Cathy Kight, was coming to shampoo and cut my hair. I was long overdue for a good haircut. She bobbed it off short, dried it and curled it and I looked and felt like a new woman. Cathy had been by to visit soon after I was transferred to St. Francis but I had missed her because I was in physical therapy. After she left I applied my make up and prepared myself for our lawyers visit concerning the accident.

I immediately got compliments from the nurses when they saw my new hair cut and that I had make-up on. It was the first time I had used my make up since the day of my transfer. I continued to have the sweating problem from the pain pills. After my meeting with the lawyers I returned to PT for the afternoon workout. Everybody there commented on my hair cut and appearance too. What a nice boost for my confidence.

February 22nd.

Kenny stayed with me last night and we talked some about the accident and my injuries. He told me it was a good thing he had not been with us for the trip because he would have told Dr. Lancourt to do whatever he had to do to save my life. It was a sobering thought for me. I wondered what I would have done had it been one of the others sitting in the "buddy seat." At that moment I knew for sure that I was glad I was the one in the seat and not my sister or any of the young men.

After Kenny left for home, it was the same old routine as far as taking my "bird bath," dressing and going to physical therapy. My first week in the new hospital with my new doctor had seemed long but so far things were going pretty well. Much better than I had expected after the disappointing first day.

When I returned from therapy my things had been moved into a private room . . . at last. My first visitor of the day was Daddy. After that it was one group of people after the other. Aunts and uncles and cousins, Helen Jo and Steve, Kenny's sister, Reba and a friend, and several members of our church family. The biggest surprise of the day was a visit from my dear friend, Rosemary, from Normal, IL. She had driven six or seven hours to see me and would turn around and drive back after her visit. All in all there were 25 visitors that day, a few of the people I had not seen in years. *And,* I had added 4 more gowns and 1 bed jacket to my collection.

Tonight was my first night without any of my family staying with me over night. I was a little nervous about it but was willing to give it a try. The thing I did not like about being alone was my total dependency on other people for all my needs. That was a scary feeling for me.

February 23rd.

No physical therapy on Sundays and that did not make me mad. Shortly after I had finished with my breakfast and bath I heard a rumbling from the hallway. It was a portable x-ray machine. The tech pushing it stopped at my door and checked his orders to be sure he had the right room. He had drafted one of the hospital security guards to help him get the machine into my room. He waited while the technician took the x-rays then helped him get the machine back out in the hall. The guard and I had chatted and really hit it off, his name was Richard Rushin and he was about the same age as my son Kent. The x-rays had been a surprise but no big deal. After they left I sat back to wait for somebody from my family to show up. Mom and Daddy were the first to arrive, closely followed by Kenny.

Later Dr. Trueblood came in to give me an update on my progress and what had to happen to get me back home, the reason for the x-rays earlier that morning. He said that first of all everything had to heal before I could be fitted for prosthesis. The biggest problem at this time was the tibia in my right leg. It was badly crushed and had a lot of building back to do. Like Dr. Lancourt he suspected that there might be a problem with that bone healing. He said my anklebone was cracked and posed a problem as well as being painful. I did not like the sound of all of that but I felt confident that our prayer warriors were still praying and it would be all right. I did not feel like God had brought me as far as He had to let me lose my right foot and leg.

After the doctor had left visitors started arriving and continued to come and go all afternoon and into the evening. There were almost as many visitors as the day before. The receptionists at the front desk said they were amazed at the amount of visitors I had. And the floor nurses commented that it was more fun to come in my room and see all the gifts I had been given than to go to Famous Barr, a local department store.

People had been so generous with flowers, potted plants, books, robes and gowns, etc. it was amazing to me also. And my card collection was growing daily.

It was good to have Kenny with me every night. It had become *our time, just* the two of us. Oh, we had been alone together in St. Joe but the difference was my condition. I was so much better now. I was not heavily medicated and in constant pain, but feeling more "normal." That night before he left he took my hand and told me how much he loved me and that he wanted me to know that my handicap made no difference to the way he felt about me. He was sorry it had happened to me, but it in no way affected his love for me or made me less attractive to him. And then he kissed me 'til my ears rang! I was convinced. I have to admit, I had wondered if my ugly legs would bother him, especially when we crawled into bed at night. He was never anything but supportive and encouraging through it all, and still is.

This was my second night without my "night watchers." I will not say I liked it, but I knew it was necessary for me to let them all go back to their beds and routines at home. I was hopeful that I would not have to be hospitalized much longer.

Kenny left around 8:30 and had only been gone a short time when I got an overwhelming feeling of loneliness. I was trying to fight it off when there was a soft knock on my door. It was Richard, the security guard, from earlier in the day. He said he just thought he would stop by to say hello and see how I was doing. We visited for a few minutes and then he was off on his way. His brief visit had gotten me through that lonely spell and not long after he left Elizabeth Colman, my RN, came and sat in my room and visited until they needed her on the floor. Several of the nurses would pop in from time to time and visit for a while. Elizabeth, Marilyn Duncan, Debbie Huckabee and Stephanie Wright were just a few of my favorites. I became especially close to the night nurses because they would come in and chat for a while after visiting hours and that helped me get through the lonely times. They were becoming very special to me just as the nurses at Heartland West had.

February 24th.

As usual, at 2:00 I was scheduled to return to physical therapy for my workout, but Dr. Trueblood came in to change my bandages and check the skin grafts. When he looked at them he did not say a word and started to leave. I thought he was going to actually leave the room without telling me about the skin grafts. As he opened the door he stopped and turned slightly around and said, "Remember the zinnias I told you about? They all came up!" Then he walked out! I was praising the Lord in my heart and spirit for I knew He had worked another miracle. The nurse told me that skin grafts rarely *all take* 100%. My legs were rebandaged and then the nurse tried to remove the bandage on the "donor site" where the skin had been taken on my left thigh. The whole bandage was stuck tight! It took 2 hours of soaking with peroxide and saline solution and little by little easing it off before they could rebandage it. Thankfully they had let me do the soaking and unsticking of the bandage.

I had a lot of visitors throughout the day. One of Mom's good friends and her sister came and when the sister saw my legs and me with the pins sticking up she burst out crying. That was a first. It was usually me crying. Poor woman was so upset she had to leave. I was sorry it had been so upsetting for her.

Once again, after Kenny left for home Richard popped in for a few minutes. He did not stay very long but he was like a breath of fresh air and just what I needed at the time. After he left Elizabeth and Kathy, both RNs came in and visited until they were needed elsewhere. God was so good to touch the hearts of these young people and send them in for short visits when I needed them most.

February 25th.

I had asked Dr. Trueblood about making an appearance at a concert in Marion, IL on the night of the 28th. Our group would be performing as the opening band for Wendy Bagwell and the Sunlighters, a group we had opened for before. I wanted to make an appearance even though I knew I could not sing. Our band had been rehearsing and Mark was going to sing my part. I thought it was important for our friends to see that I was truly okay. Battered, but okay. Dr. Trueblood said he would think about it.

After lunch we used my parents car to practice my transferring from the wheel chair to the back seat of their car using the transfer board. Then back out of the car and into the wheel chair. I had been told that I would soon be allowed to go home on weekends and this was an important part of preparing for that. I also knew I would need to know how to enter and exit the car if I got to attend the concert the 28th. I wanted to go to that concert in the worst way! I made the transfer in and out without too much trouble, although the pins sticking up were the biggest problem. It was not an easy thing to do, but I did it with the help of the others and I was pretty happy about that. Afterward I went back into the gym to finish my workout. Mom and Daddy sat and watched for a while before going back to my room to wait for me. After I finished Barb told me I could go on back to my room myself if I wanted to. Another first. I took off a bit reluctantly, hoping I had paid enough attention to all of the twists and turns between physical therapy and the orthopedic wing of the hospital to find my way back to my room. As I was wheeling along I heard Freida behind me pushing another patient in his wheel chair. She followed me and encouraged me and I made it just fine. What Freida did not know was, about halfway back to my room I was ready to drop, but I was too stubborn to let her see me quit. I was not used to wheeling myself yet and that was quite a long distance for my first time. I was worn out.

February 26th.

I had gotten into the habit of listening to scripture cassettes at night as I was settling down to go to sleep. I used headphones, and more times than not, I would wake up with them still in place the next morning. The scriptures gave me comfort and peace as I drifted off to sleep and kept my mind from dwelling on my condition or the pain.

In physical therapy Barb and I had been working on trying to get my foot from the "drop foot" position to a 90-degree angle. Until we accomplished that a cast could not be put on that leg and foot. The way we worked on it was by putting a towel or sheet under the arch and pulling back as far and as hard as I could stand it. Barb had gotten it to -5 degrees today and we had started with it at -20 degrees. It hurt something awful but it had to be done. She asked me to work on it in my room in the evenings also.

My boys visited tonight. It was actually after visiting hours when they arrived but the nurses were pretty lenient with my family. Kenny was already there and the three of them stayed until 9:15. After they left two of my nurses came in to visit for a while as usual. There were times when I would have three nurses in my room after Kenny left, it just depended on how busy they were and how many patients were on the floor.

February 27th.

In the morning physical therapy session I went through my usual routine with weights then Barb came over to help me work on my foot again. We got it to -10 degrees and then in the afternoon session we got it to a -5 degrees again, same as yesterday. It really, really hurt and twice when she pulled it back I nearly cried. She looked me right in the eye and said, "You must have a very high pain tolerance because I know that had to *really* hurt." She did not know how close to tears I was at that point. After she had gotten it to -5 she had me work on it more with a sheet, which was a little easier than with a towel.

I got word that I could attend the concert the next night! Picture me grinning from ear to ear because I was. There had been speculation that Dr. Trueblood might let me go home after the concert and spend the weekend there. However, he said he wanted me to come back to the hospital afterwards. That was okay. Doing all of it in one weekend might have been too much. Going home would be next and I could wait.

Helen Jo and Mom washed my hair and Cathy, my stylist, came and dried it and curled it. They had it looking very pretty again in preparation for the concert the next night.

Kenny had continued to stay with me every night until 8:30 or 9:00. I was doing pretty well on my own after he left because my nurses and Richard were always checking on me. My insecurity had lessened after I had learned to transfer in and out of the bed and wheel chair using the transfer board. I did not feel as dependent on others as I had. Who would have thought a well-varnished piece of wood about the size of a skateboard would be such a wonderful tool.

I was still taking a couple of Tylenol 3's and a pain pill at night to sleep. Having to sleep on my back in the same position all night had been difficult to get accustomed to, as well as sleeping with my legs elevated on pillows. The Tylenol and pain pill along with my Bible scripture cassettes helped me deal with it.

February 28th.

The bandages were changed, and my legs and foot looked good. There was still a lot of swelling in them but not nearly like they were in St. Joe. The wounds were healing very well since the skin grafts. The donor site was still sore and itchy but was healing. The bandage changes were not as bad as they had been in the beginning but I always dreaded them.

After my afternoon physical therapy I went back to my room and started getting ready for the trip to Marion. Kenny and Daddy had come to get me, but I ran them out while I bathed and dressed in a pink gown and robe. To cover my legs, Helen Jo had sent a beautiful hand crocheted afghan that had big pink roses on it.

It took 3 or 4 to get me in the car but no harm was done and we were on our way. The drive to Marion Civic Center was a little over an hour and I enjoyed the ride. It was very good to be out and about. I was a little nervous about going but my excitement was bigger than my nervousness.

The Civic Center was packed—SOLD OUT—with 1,100 in attendance. It was tricky getting me out of the car and into the wheel chair but we managed to do it. Kenny took me in the back door while Daddy parked the car. Sandy Stevenson was waiting for me back stage. I think she had appointed herself as my personal "body guard" that night and would have decked anybody who tried to bother me. There were many hugs back stage. Geraldine, one of the women who sang with Wendy Bagwell, was especially sweet to me. And Sandy was by my side every minute. When it was time for the concert to begin Dean Stevenson took his place on stage as MC. After a few minutes of warming up the crowd he introduced The Galatians and they took their places on stage. Then he introduced me. Wendy Bagwell pushed my wheel chair out to the middle of the stage and Helen Jo met me with a beautiful bouquet of sweetheart roses. I have been told I was given a standing ovation that lasted 3 minutes. Naturally, I cried and cried. It was difficult to get myself straightened up enough to say a few words to the people but I managed to do it. I don't have a clue what I said but I'm certain it included thanks to the people for their love and prayers. After I had finished speaking Wendy wheeled me back stage. Just as we got to the edge of the stage he leaned over by my right ear and in his Smyrna, Georgia accent said, "Honey, you tore that crowd up!" I had to laugh. Later when Wendy and the ladies were singing Geraldine dedicated a song to me and I cried again. It was a very emotional night with lots of tears. Wendy has gone on to Heaven now, but I look forward to seeing him again up there. He was a very special man.

The Galatians did an outstanding job of singing and playing music that night and it only made me more determined than ever to get back out there again. I never thought I would be on the stage 35 days after the wreck but there I was. I wondered to what point 35 more days would bring me. Would my voice still be weak and hoarse? Would that problem go away and my voice become normal and strong again? Would I really be able to walk on stage again? There were so many questions going through my mind. Many things for me to think about on the ride back to the hospital.

I had enjoyed having many visitors back stage, but it surprised me as we were leaving the Civic Center, when the car was swarmed with people all around it. They just wanted me to know they loved me and were glad to see me. Another tug on my emotions but it was a wonderful night and I had loved every minute of it. I wondered what Dr. Lancourt would have thought about that night. After his question about me being a celebrity when he saw all of the flowers I had received in St. Joe, I thought he might have been pleased with my brief celebrity treatment.

On the way back to the hospital we went through a drive-through for burgers and sodas. I had not had anything to eat or drink since noon. It would have been a problem to get me to a rest room and I felt it was better to abstain. However, just in case there was a need my ever-thoughtful sister had brought a bedpan. Thankfully there was no need for that hated thing!

When I got to St. Francis it was 11:20. My nurse, Stephanie Wright, told me I was grounded 2 weeks for being 20 minutes late. All of my nurses were very happy for me that I had gotten to go to the concert. They knew what it meant to me.

March 1st.

Shirley and Carole, the two ladies who had sent me the pretty little plant in St. Joe, the one that I wondered how long it would take me to kill, had been at the concert the night before. They live a good distance away and my parents had invited them to spend the weekend with them. They all came to visit me at the hospital and then went shopping. I hated to miss out on that!

March 2nd.

Dr. Trueblood came in to see my legs during the bandage change and pin care. He said, "Looks good." Patted me on the shoulder and said, "You're gonna be all right." I had come to like him better all the time. He was very funny in a dry sort of way and was always kidding about something. He had also begun volunteering things about his children and their dog. I have tried to remember the dog's name but can only remember it was unusual for a dog. It was Elizabeth Ann, or something like that.

The nurse had given me the news earlier that I could go home on pass for the day. What a surprise that was. I had thought I might get to go the next weekend but not this one since I had gone to the concert the night before.

I would be going to Mom and Dad's because our house was in need of a good cleaning. Kenny and Daddy came after me around 11:00 and we loaded up and headed for Olive Branch. It had been 36 days since I had seen my home. Though I would not go to it this time, we would be passing by as we went to my parents. When we got there Kenny and Daddy carried me in the house. I can't describe the feeling I got when we went inside. I don't think anybody realized it but I was overwhelmed with the feeling that I did not know how to act or what to do with myself. It was totally unexpected. I really wanted to have a good cry but I did not want to do that and upset everyone. And then I found myself wondering how I would handle everything when I got home and if I would be able to do *anything*. I felt wounded and hurt. It was not feelings of self-pity even though that is how it sounds. It was a heartache. It is difficult to describe all of the different emotions, feelings and thoughts that were overwhelming me. Part of it was that I have always been very independent. Now I was so dependent on others and it was a totally new thing for me. And I did not like it. I knew I could and would handle all of it. However, when it all hit at once and overwhelmed, it was hard to deal with. That was just one of the "bad moments" I had from time to time and I knew it would pass.

Kenny had walked to our house, which was just two houses down from my parent's house, so he could get out of the crowd and rest for a while. Daddy and Mom wanted to take Shirley and Carole for a little tour of our area and as soon as the car left the driveway I told Helen Jo that I had to go to the bathroom. We both knew this was going to be a problem but we would figure it out. My parent's bathroom is small and we were not sure the wheel chair would even go in. It did, just barely, it had to be backed in and positioned in front of the commode and the arm removed from the chair so I could use the transfer board and slide to the pot. All without falling in or dunking my clothing. Our first attempt was less than perfect. The biggest problem was that the commode was several inches lower than the seat of the wheel chair and that made using the transfer board difficult. After a round of giggling I finally managed to make the transfer to the stool and then realized that I had not pulled my pants down. By this time we were nearly hysterical with laughter over the whole situation, especially when I almost fell into the pot trying to correct my clothing mistake. After the deed was finally accomplished, it was a matter of doing everything in reverse, which brought on another round of laughter. By the time everybody came back to the house we were pictures of innocence sitting in the living room. However, it had been just the thing I had needed to break the mood I had been experiencing the first hour I was there.

Later that evening Kenny and Daddy took me back to the hospital. It had been a good day and I had enjoyed the outing but I was tired and ready for my bed.

March 3rd.

Dr. Trueblood came in and asked the nurse to take the bandages off my legs so he could see them. His timing had been a little off; this would be the second bandage change of the day. He said they looked real good and then told me to get x-rays after physical therapy. He wanted Barb and I to work on getting my foot in a neutral position. Now that the open wounds had nearly healed from the skin grafting, he was thinking about the next surgery, which would be to remove the pins and put casts on both legs. My foot would have to be in the right position by then.

March 6th.

I got to go home to Mom's for 5 days before my next surgery. Mom and Helen Jo had the huge job of cleaning up my house. They said it was awful! There was mail and newspapers 2 feet deep on the kitchen table. Of course, women see "clean" a bit differently than most men. From what they told me I think it was more cluttered than anything. But, the fact remained it had not been cleaned since before the accident on January 25th. They had started the cleaning job but did not have time to finish. They had also realized that furniture would have to be rearranged to accommodate the wheel chair. It was easier for me to go to Mom and

Dad's for this first 5-day pass. The boys had been on their own since the accident and although they had kept the dishes washed up and their laundry done, that was about all they could handle. While we were still in St. Joe someone had come in and showed Kent and Mark how to run the washer and dryer so they could wash their clothes. My three men had *never* had to do any of those things until after January 25th. They had gotten a crash course in taking care of themselves and they had done well and I was proud of them.

My little buddy, Matt, visited me several times while I was at Mom's. He would sit beside me when I was lying on the couch and just keep me company. He had seen a little more of the injuries to my legs when he watched his mom clean the pin sites. It did not seem to bother him and he never said a lot about them, at least not to me. I have found through the years that children are much more accepting of handicaps than most adults. My grandson Jacob has been curious about my legs since he was big enough to understand that my legs and feet were different. I never hid them from him and therefore it is quite natural as far as he is concerned. From time to time he has asked to see them and I always let him look and inspect. The last time, at the age of 5, he looked both legs and the half-foot over thoroughly and then he said, "That's really bad Daw Daw." Then he handed me my prosthetic leg and was ready for me to put it on and go play with him. When he was old enough to understand I told him that when I got to Heaven some day God would put my feet back. He thought that was "way cool." Now and then he reminds me of that. As my youngest grandson Ethan gets older I expect he too will have questions and do his own inspections. I also expect that he will handle it just fine.

March 11th.

Monday, Barbara and I finally got my foot into a neutral position. It was a lot of work and very painful but we did it! Today was surgery #6 to remove the Hoffman Pins and put plaster casts on both legs. Kenny took pictures of my legs without the bandages before surgery and the casts were put on. After the film was developed the pictures were sent to Dr. Lancourt so he could see how my legs were healing. The pin sites had been a constant source of pain and irritation from the beginning, not to mention the aggravating problem with the braces on top locking together when I forgot and let them get too close together. I was glad to be rid of them and sincerely hoped it was my last surgery.

When I woke up after surgery I was shocked at the weight of the casts. They were extremely heavy, wet and very warm! I had never worn a cast before and did not know that it would take them several hours to dry. They had brought in lights to help speed the drying process. The left cast was uncomfortable because it was 3 or 4 inches above the knee and prevented my knee from bending. I assumed it had to be that way to help it stay on. There was an artificial foot bolted to the bottom of the cast. The right cast was below the knee and fairly comfortable.

March 12th.

The left cast continued to be very uncomfortable, not only because of the above-the-knee position of the cast but it was hurting at the fracture site on the shin. Never the less, I went to physical therapy for my workouts. Barb had told me that morning that she wanted me to try to walk in the afternoon session. Mom, Helen Jo, Kent and Mark were all there to watch me. I was positioned between the parallel bars and pulled myself up on my feet. Barb asked me to try to take a step and I did. That was about the point where I lost Kent and Mark. I took two more steps before I had to sit down. Victory was mine! It had hurt like heck but it felt wonderful to be upright again, actually standing.

After my first step Kent and Mark had left. They could not stand to see me doing something that they knew had to be *very* painful. Kenny had told me that Mark was having a hard time dealing with everything anyway. He had talked with his Dad about it and he just could not understand how I was ever going to be able to cope with my handicap. I don't know for sure how Kent felt about it. I do know he had seen far too much in the stair well that morning when he saw my legs and feet. I think maybe he thought I would be able to cope. Perhaps because he was older he knew how tough I was. After all, that morning in the ER he was the one who had asked Helen Jo which foot was totally gone. When she said the left he had said, "Good, she can still drive." From that statement I think Kent fully expected me to overcome.

Helen Jo called Dr. Lancourt to give him an update since my last surgery, the removal of the pins and addition of plaster casts. After they chatted for a few minutes he told her that it was a good thing we had come through and needed a doctor when we did, because he was leaving St. Joe. He would be moving to Dallas, Texas to open his new practice the end of June or first of May. He told her he would be on his own this time and he thought it was time. Then he asked about my progress and me. His first question was whether or not I had lost the other four or five inches off my left leg. She told him that I had not lost any additional inches and that I had been up on my feet that day. He was thrilled to hear that. She said he was still curious about Dr. Trueblood and wanted to know if he was human and if he had a personality. She assured him that he was and did. Then he said, "I want to share with you what I've been chuckling about for all these weeks." He said, "I'm Jewish." She told him she had found that out. He went on to say that he had thought it funny that she had asked him all about his beliefs, to which his answers were all, "No," then let him go ahead and take care of me. She said, "What you didn't know was that I had asked God for not just *any doctor* but *His best*. And at that point I felt we had gotten His best." (He did not know what the nurse had told her in ER that morning.) She asked about Dick and he said he had been invited to go to Dallas with him but Dick's wife was not happy about moving. He said Dick thought they might follow in a couple of months. Helen Jo told him they worked so well together it would be a shame if Dick did not join him. He asked if we ever sang in Texas. She told him that we had and hoped to again in the future. Before they hung up he told her, "Keep singing and keep talkin'!" His parting statement was confirmation that he had come to admire her spirit and spunk that morning when she challenged him about taking my legs off. If she had not done the "talkin'" I would not be walking today. And I will forever be grateful for her intercession on my behalf.

March 13th & 14th.

I walked again in physical therapy. I could not take very many steps at a time but it had been such a sense of accomplishment for me.

The pain at the fracture site had not gotten better and because I continued to complain about it, Dr. Trueblood had me taken to x-ray to find out what the problem was. As it turned out the metal prongs holding the plate the artificial foot was bolted to, was not padded enough and was gouging my leg. The man who would be making my prosthesis was called to come to the hospital and cut the defective cast off and put a new one on. I was glad the problem had been found but did not look forward to the cast procedure again.

The man from the prosthetics lab came in with a full sized man's artificial leg (thigh, lower leg and foot) and flopped it on the other bed in my room. He said he thought I might like to see what a prosthesis looked like. To me the prosthesis looked like it was as big as I was and I nearly died! On the inside I was wishing I could run away and I was very close to tears but I would bet that he never had a clue how I was feeling. Don't get me wrong, he was a very nice man and I liked him but I did not like the manner in which I was introduced to prosthesis. He went about his business of cutting the defective cast off and putting the new one on. It felt better from the start because it had a cutout under the knee, which made it easier to bend my leg. And, no more prongs inside gouging my leg. It felt so much better, even wet and heavy, that I forgave him for his rather crude introduction to artificial legs. But I will never forget it!

March 20th.

I had asked for and received a pass to go home and practice with our band. We were scheduled to perform at the Southern Illinois Quartet Convention the 22nd. It was always held at the Marion Civic Center, the very place I had made my first appearance on the 28th of February. This would be the first time I had sung since before our accident fifty-seven days earlier. I felt it was a bit of a record that I had come far enough in less than two months to participate in a concert. I was excited, but nervous too. I would have to sit in the wheel chair, which was very restrictive. In our concerts the four singers all moved around on the stage and interacted with each other and those in the band. I would not be able to do that in the wheel chair. I was also very concerned about the hoarseness and weakness in my voice. Practice went very well although we could see right away that Mark would need to back me up on my tenor part to give it strength.

I returned to the hospital that night after practice and spent the night and next day doing my usual routine. That evening I went home again on another pass for the whole weekend. I had to be back at the hospital on Sunday night but Dr. Trueblood had said I might be released on Monday or Tuesday to go home for good.

March 21st 22nd.

The concert was great! Although my voice was still weak and hoarse I did better than I had expected. I'm sure prayer had a lot to do with that. It also helped knowing Mark was backing me up. I was able to relax because he was giving strength where I did not have it. I got another standing ovation, which I had not expected but certainly appreciated. Everyone was so wonderful. Although I had used my wheel chair on stage, when we went to the dressing rooms, which were downstairs, I used my walker. The other performers were surprised to see me walking. After the concert, I promised myself that I would not sing from the wheel chair *ever* again. I would bring a stool to prop on or something, but I would not use the wheel chair again. I did not like that feeling of restriction at all.

After the concert many came by the record table to shake hands and give encouraging words. Someone asked if they could sign one of my casts and from there it snowballed into several taking a turn. They seemed to get a kick out of it and it was fun for me too. Business was good for the sale of our new promotional picture, which had been taken not long before the accident, and we signed many autographs.

From Marion we drove to Olive Branch and home. It was very good to be in my own home, for the weekend. Mom and Helen Jo had gotten the house whipped into shape and rearranged the furniture in the living room for more room when I was in the wheel chair. I was using the walker almost exclusively, but there would be times when I had to use my wheels. I felt especially liberated since I could walk. I could get around so much better, use the bathroom much easier, get dressed easier, etc. I had been told that walking would help stimulate the bones and help the healing process, and I was going to walk as much as I could. Healed bones were what I wanted as soon as possible. Oh, it was painful, but I had already experienced much worse.

My leg wounds and pin sites on the left leg were all healed and looked good. The last night I was at home I discovered quite accidentally that the left cast would slip off. I had "lost" it in bed and was horrified! No damage had been done and I just slipped it back on as if it were a boot, but it was scary. The fracture site still pained me but the swelling had gone down in the leg a lot. Thus the slip-off cast. As soon as the fracture completely healed I would be fitted with a prosthetic leg and foot. The right leg was healing much more slowly because of the one-inch gap where the bone had been crushed. Dr. Trueblood had said that I would have to wear a cast on the right leg much longer than the left. I would not mind as long as it healed.

March 23rd & 24th.

After the weekend at home I went back to the hospital on Sunday night as expected. I followed my usual routine and physical therapy sessions. Around 4:00 PM Dr. Trueblood came in and told me he was releasing me from the hospital. I could go home. Helen Jo was there with me and she took off to rent a wheel chair and walker and pick up my prescriptions. She had just left when Kenny arrived. Thank goodness he was there to help load everything into the cars. I had taken a lot of my things home on Friday, only keeping necessities at the hospital, in anticipation of my release. There was not as much to load as there could have been. It felt very good to know that I would not have to check back into the hospital after a couple of days at home. I was home to stay after 6 surgeries and 8 weeks of nearly constant hospitalization. I had a long way to go yet, prosthesis to learn to use, and a handicap to learn to deal with but going home was good. I had been told that after I graduated from the wheel chair and walker I would use two canes to help me walk, and then eventually I might be able to only use one cane. That was okay, whatever it took to get me more "normal." I would be returning to St. Francis for physical therapy on Tuesdays and Thursdays for a while.

Early on in my physical therapy sessions Barbara had mentioned that later on I would be getting gait training and probably occupational therapy. I did not even know what those two things were. At first I thought it was "gate" training and that made no sense whatsoever. I knew how to go in and out of a gate. Then I found out that the word was "gait" which has to do with the way a person walks. Gait training was to teach me how to walk with the prosthesis, training I never needed. Another miracle? I do not doubt it. Occupational therapy was to teach me how to manage in my home, cooking, doing laundry, etc. I never needed that either.

March 25.

This was the two-month anniversary of our accident. Helen Jo took me to St. Francis for my hour of outpatient physical therapy. When we returned

I spent the day trying to organize all of the things I had been given in the hospital. I had a huge basket of cards and letters . . . nearly 600. There were 28 plants, which had to be divided between Mom, Helen Jo and me. I did not have room for that many plants and there was no way I could ever keep them alive with my brown thumb. The rearrangement of the living room helped a lot as far as my getting around. Daddy and Mom had bought a small television with a remote control for me to have in the living room. Our own television was in the family room and it was down 2 steps. I would not be venturing there for a while. Helen Jo was going to cook dinner for her family and mine at my home and we would all eat together until I was more stable on my feet and could cook for my family. I would help her with things I could do in a sitting position. It would be a while before we could all get back to a more normal home life, but we were so much closer than we had been.

The next day, Wednesday, we went shopping and I used my walker at each stop we made, except for Wal-Mart where they had the wheel chair carts. If I remember correctly, that was where Mom pushed me through a rack of clothing. Not on purpose, of course, but the racks were so close together she just plowed through like a Sherman Tank and unfortunately I was in the lead. The outing was very tiring and I was worn out when I got home, but I enjoyed it.

March 27th.

We went to St. Francis for my hour of physical therapy and then on to the Prosthetics Lab where I was measured for my first prosthesis for the left leg. The measuring was not a problem, but the plaster he put on my leg to make the form for the prosthesis was kind of rough. It was an actual plaster cast. He dipped a roll of plaster-coated gauze in a bucket of water and then began wrapping my leg making it conform to every bump and ridge. After it dried it was pulled off. That was the rough part. With the fracture site still quite tender, as well as other areas on my leg, it was a bit uncomfortable. The prosthesis would be ready for a fitting in a couple of weeks. I was taking the old cast off all of the time because the bones and wounds were all healed and with a lot of the swelling gone I was wearing it like a boot. After all, it had the prosthetic foot on it and without it I could not have walked.

March 30th.

There was a church in St. Louis, The Cathedral at the Crossroads, where we had sung many times. We considered the pastor, Rev. James Drysdale, our pastor and the congregation our church family. They had come to see me in the hospital in Cape a couple of times and we were anxious to see all of them again. I was especially anxious for them to see me on my feet. Their prayers were a big part of the miracle that I was. We decided to make the two and a half hour drive there for the Easter morning service. When I walked in the front door one of the precious black women was in the vestibule. When she saw me she started shouting and dancing and having a big old hallelujah spell. When she finally got her shoutin' over she grabbed me and bear hugged me! She was short and she was round and when she hugged you, you knew it! And I loved it. It was much the same when the others saw us walking in. Brother Lay, the music director, sang my favorite song GOD WILL MAKE A WAY. He sang it directly to me and I was very touched by it. I had always loved to hear him sing that particular song.

We were invited to Pastor Drysdale and Darlene's home for lunch after morning service. We ate, visited and relaxed until 3:00 then headed back home. It had been a wonderful day and I made the trip fine, but I was worn out when we got back home. I knew it would take at least an hour for my legs to settle down enough for me to sleep when I got home. I was still taking a pain pill at bedtime but had quit all of the other medication the doctor had me on. Some of it was making me gain weight and I knew I did not need extra weight to carry around on my healing legs.

April 2nd.

Yesterday was Matthew's 4th birthday. Helen Jo baked a cake for him and we had a little party. I was amazed at how well he had accepted everything. Naturally he was interested and curious about my legs but he just took it in stride.

April 3rd.

Today it was back to physical therapy as usual. I had Barb check my right leg. We had noticed that it seemed bowed. The cast was also loose and my foot was turning out like a ducks foot. Barb called Dr. Trueblood and told him about it and he wanted to see me the next day at 1:00.

The next day at Dr. Trueblood's office I was taken to x-ray first thing. When he viewed the x-rays he explained that the tibia, though healing, was drifting toward the fibula. The fibula being stronger, was keeping the tibia from healing properly, which was causing the leg to bow out. Corrective procedure was to make a small incision and cut the fibula then both bones would heal together and correctly. Surgery was scheduled for Tuesday the 8th at 10:30. So much for being finished with surgeries. This would be #7.

As they prepared me for surgery I reminded the anesthesiologist about the tube down my throat causing hoarseness and that I was a singer. He promised he would remember and use a smaller tube.

The surgery went as expected but I once again had a terrible headache that lasted all day. It seemed the headaches were from the anesthetic but I did not understand why I did not have them after *every* surgery. One of my favorite nurses, Beth was on duty and took very good care of me. Dr. Trueblood said I could go home as soon as I felt like it and I checked out of the hospital on Wednesday afternoon.

April 10th.

On the way to physical therapy this morning I got another bad headache, which got worse while I was in my session. I was scheduled to go to the Prosthetic Lab to try on my temporary left prosthesis after therapy and although I really did not feel like going, I went on because I was anxious to get the leg and begin learning how to walk with it. When I was taken into the room for the fitting the first thing I saw was the leg leaning against the wall with my shoe on the foot. It seemed huge and ugly and there were straps to fasten it on, all of which were very cumbersome. As I was trying it on for the first time, the prosthetist told me that I would not be able to wear jeans or anything very tight because of the straps that held the leg on. Once again I had that feeling of wanting to run away. I was walking with the leg and the prosthetist was making adjustments as we went along when about half way through the fitting we had to quit because my head was hurting so badly. I would have to come back another day for further adjustments. I just wanted out of there and to go home. The walking I had done during the fitting was surprisingly easy. Much easier walking than with the cast. It felt a little lighter weight even though I was told it weighed three pounds. John Tipler, a big black man with a smile full of white teeth, pushed my wheel chair to the car. He told me he worked in the back where the prosthetics were made. On the way to the car he asked me if I was still singing for Jesus. I told him I was and he started praying for me in another language. As he helped me into the car he said, "You never know when you will run into one of us, do you? We're everywhere." And he had that big old smile on his face. I don't know how he knew I was a Spirit filled Christian or that I was a Gospel singer, but I knew we were kindred spirits. I almost felt like I had experienced an encounter with an angel. I was very blessed by his prayer and his happy spirit.

April 15th.

We had received a call from a Christian radio station about coming for an interview. I decided that I probably should not go because of the distance and late evening hour of the program. Steve and Helen Jo were asked if they would consider being interviewed even though I would not be there. We were all listening at home and were proud of the good job they did answering the host's questions and telling our story.

Over the last few days things had settled into a routine of sorts. Though I could do very little and had to rest a lot I was still glad to be back in my home. Now and then I would have a bad day. I had too much idle time to think and wonder about the future. When Kenny and I got into bed that night I had a "melt-down." I started crying and could not stop. Kenny just held me and let me cry it out. I hated being maimed and it bothered me most when I would get into bed with my husband. He had assured me over and over that he loved me and my handicap did not change that. I believed him and had not expected him to be any other way. However, it bothered me *for* him.

Now that I was at home, I was finding my boys were also very supportive. Mark was especially interested in my legs and the prosthesis. He had been curious about how it worked, felt, etc. Right after the accident he had been very disturbed about my loss and talked with Kenny several times about it. Kenny said he kept asking, "How will Mom possibly handle the loss of her feet?" In one of our talks, he told me about seeing the blood in the stairwell of the bus that morning. He said there was so much it scared him. I had also learned that when he, Kent and Brad were sitting in the Police car after I had been taken to the hospital, they had heard the dispatcher say that both of my legs had been amputated. They had to be so scared.

Kent did not seem to be as interested in seeing my legs at that time but that did not surprise me. He had always been a bit squeamish about such things and after what he had seen when he was trying to help me get unpinned I'm sure it was enough horror for a lifetime. He had told me that my legs were crossed below the knees and there was metal and wood all twisted in and around them.

As the swelling went down in the right leg the cast had to be changed about once a month. When I would see my leg after the old cast was cut off, it would shock me at how gross it looked. It was even worse than the left one had been. The hair had grown long and there were dead skin cells on the whole leg. I never knew I had that much hair on my legs . . . I decided that the casts were like hair hot houses! Every time I saw that mess I wanted to say, "Hey, let's clean this thing up a little before you put the new cast on!" After the left cast was taken off for good I did clean that leg up. I scrubbed it until the dead skin cells were all gone and my skin was pink and normal looking again. And then I shaved the long hair and pampered my leg with body lotion. When I went to PT the next time and Barb saw that I had shaved my leg she was horrified! She said, "Deanna, you are not supposed to shave your leg when you wear a prosthesis!" I said, "Now, Barb, you needn't think that I won't shave my legs!" She just shook her head and did not say another word. I promised her I would always be very careful. I never did find out why you are not supposed to shave the leg you wear a prosthesis on. I figured it was probably because of cuts and possible infection. I was always very careful and it was such an improvement it was worth it.

April 17th.

It was still very painful to walk but I kept at it knowing it was good for the bones. When I had walked a lot on the days I went to physical therapy and the Prosthetic Lab, I would rest a lot the next day. I would be glad when the physical therapy sessions ended and we did not have to make that trip twice a week to Cape. Since I had the surgery to cut the fibula bone I was experiencing a lot of additional pain at the fracture site. I could only hope that meant it was healing as expected. The next Thursday I would go back to Dr. Trueblood to have the cast taken off and the staples taken out of the incision. I got so tired of hurting and I hated being such a drag on everyone. I was impatient to get back to normal at home as well as back on the road singing.

April 21st.

Last Friday night our group practiced here at our house. My voice was still weak and tended to get hoarse pretty fast, but it was getting better. However, I continued to wonder if it would ever be the same again.

Kent, Helen Jo and Steve went to Nashville and met with Ronny Hinson and Ron Drake about finishing the album we had started before the accident. I wanted to go with them so badly but thought the three and a half hour drive down and then three and a half hours back would have been too much and I stayed home.

April 24th.

I went to Dr. Trueblood's office today and they x-rayed my right leg, cut a "window" in the cast over the incision and removed the staples through the window. After they were removed they filled the window in with gauze and then used two rolls of plaster gauze over it to hold it all in place, which increased the bulk of the cast. It felt like it weighed seven or eight pounds. It was impossible to wear slacks or jeans for the cast changes and prosthetic fittings and the wide legged split skirts I had recently found worked very well.

April 28th.

Helen Jo had applied for a job in an oral surgeon's office. If she got it I would really miss her. She had been my right arm and both legs for the past three months. Perhaps it would be good for her to have a diversion from all of this. I was hoping I would be able to do my own cooking and cleaning, etc. before too long.

We had decided to have a yard sale the first of May. I had doubts about ever being able to do that sort of thing again but I thought I could handle it. I could at least be the cashier and that was more fun anyway!

May 3rd.

We all loaded up and went to see Gold City, one of our favorite Gospel Quartets, tonight. They sang in a parking lot at a shopping center about an hour north of us. They were surprised to see Steve walking toward them and then when he told them I was there, here they all came. I think they were as glad to see us, as we were to see them. The concert was great and then we enjoyed a good visit with them at a local restaurant afterwards over dinner.

May 4th.

We sang twice in Missouri. The first concert was at 1:30 and the second at 6:00. Mom had made a long skirt and matching top for me to wear. With the cast and all, clothing had been a problem. However, I was more self conscious about the ugly prosthesis than I was the cast. The artificial leg was so big and the ankle twice as big around as my natural ankle had been. I hoped that in the future the leg would be smaller and more natural looking. I wore a flat shoe on the artificial foot but the right half-foot was still in a cast. We had a good day but it was very tiring for me and my legs were aching terribly when we got back home.

Helen Jo was scheduled to start working for the oral surgeon the 5th. It was only part time while one of the secretaries was on maternity leave. I hoped it would be a good job for her and something she would enjoy. There was a possibility it could become permanent. I knew I would really miss her during the day. I was so used to her popping in and out of my house it would seem strange without that.

We had been talking a lot about the concerts we had on the books for the upcoming months. The 16th we had one in North Carolina with the Easter Brothers and on the 17th one in Pennsylvania at a Christian supper club. We planned to rent a van in order to keep those two bookings. Without the comforts of a bus for long trips it was difficult to know what to do.

May 13.

I had an appointment with Dr. Trueblood for a cast change. The new one was a lot smaller than the last had been. Not so big and cumbersome. He told me the x-rays showed several bone fragments at the crush-site on the tibia but it was filling in with calcium and looked to be healing well. He pushed and pulled on my leg and said it was pretty stable now. I was really glad of that! When he started pushing and pulling on it I expected it to hurt or fall apart. He also said that my foot was in a neutral position and that was very good. Thank God Barb and I were able to accomplish that in physical therapy. Dr. Trueblood put the new cast on my leg because he wanted to be sure the foot was kept in that neutral position. While he was working on the cast he turned and looked at Mom and said, "Isn't she cute?" During past visits he had also told me two or three times, "You are a remarkable lady." I never knew what was going to come out of his mouth, if it would be serious or funny. He had continued to chat about his kids and their dog. He was nothing like Dr. Lancourt, their personalities were totally different, but I liked him and so far he was doing great. His office nurse, Helen, had told Mom, "Deanna has set some records and broken some with her recovery." More and more I was realizing the miracle that I was and what God had done for me.

May 15th.

Literally, tonight at the last minute we had to cancel the North Carolina and Pennsylvania bookings. We had to face the fact that there was not enough room in a van to travel in anything close to comfort with seven people, our luggage and necessary equipment. It was a low moment for all of us.

I had been doing my own laundry for the last week or so. I was also cooking some. I could sit on the step stool and do several things in the kitchen. I still was not able to do much cleaning. Mom had been keeping the living room and kitchen cleaned but the bedrooms and bathrooms were beginning to need a good going over.

May 26th.

We went to a dinner today where there were several family members and close friends. It was nice and I enjoyed visiting with everyone but I think some were a bit uncomfortable and unsure how to act around me. The little kids were fine. They came running to me and wanted to know how I was and chattered away. The old folks were okay too, hugged my neck and told me how glad they were to see me. However it was obvious some of the ones my own age were uncomfortable. I had experienced that reaction several times lately. I did not understand why they reacted that way. I was still the same person I had been before January 25th; I was just a bit handicapped now.

May 27th.

Our John Deere Dealership closed its doors today. Kenny was now without a job and we had no income. With the farm economy at an all time low, the dealership had been in trouble and barely afloat before the accident. To that point Kenny had been keeping it's head above water with sheer guts and will power. After our accident he told his employees he did not know what he would find when he got to St. Joseph, but he would be in touch with them as soon as he could. When he arrived at the hospital and learned the extent of my injuries, he called the store and told his employees of my condition. He also told them he had to be with me and did not know when he would be able to return. It would be over a month before he got back to check on the business and there was no saving it after that. Our lawyers were advising us to take bankruptcy but Kenny said he had not been raised that way and refused. And then we found out that when a business goes belly-up some, no; most of the people who owed it money did not feel they had to pay their bills. As a result, that threw us into a lawsuit with John Deere over what was owed to them . . . because the people who had purchased equipment were not paying us, we could not pay John Deere. In the long run Kenny took all of the unpaid bills, the ones owed to the store, to the fireplace and burned them. He said if he did not turn loose of them it would drive him crazy. And we did eventually pay off everything owed to John Deere.

June 1.

We went through the 13 concerts we had booked for June and the ones, which were more than a couple of hours away were canceled, three in Tennessee, three in Arkansas and three in Texas. Another low time for all of us. We had been so close to realizing our dream and now had almost come to a stand still. We would continue to sing within a couple of hours of our area. Anything farther than that would be too uncomfortable and tiring, not only for me but everyone.

We continued to receive long distance calls from friends in Nebraska, Arkansas, Georgia and other states as well as locally wanting updates on my progress. Additional cards and letters arrived daily. I was glad to know people had not forgotten and continued to pray.

June 6th.

We sang tonight at Hurst, IL, a small town a little over an hour north of home. I had been standing for the concerts now but continued to carry my step stool to prop on or sit on for a minute to rest my legs. It was the very stool Mark had used when he was too small to hold the bass for a full concert. I felt much better standing so I could move around a little using the mic stand for support and interact with the others on the stage. A much more normal feeling.

June 19th.

I went back to Dr. Trueblood's for my monthly check up and another new cast. I figured I had had so many at that point I had probably bought a barrel of plaster. Each new cast required 24 hours of drying time during which I had to stay off of it. Of course, it was very heavy and very warm when it was wet. It would not be a bad thing in the wintertime however, in mid June it lost it's appeal.

I had settled into something of a routine in the last few weeks. I had been doing all of our cooking. I even made chicken and dumplings one night. I think it aggravated Mom that I had done it all by myself. She rather huffily told me she would have made chicken and dumplings for me. Of course, I knew that, but I wanted to do it myself. I had to wash my dishes by hand because my old dishwasher had died just before we left January 24th. Not a good time to be without a dishwasher but I was making it okay. Some of the simplest tasks were a real challenge. The first time I made our bed I felt like I had run a race and won! I was quite proud of each new accomplishment.

July 3rd.

We had a few local concerts on the books for July. One was today in Jackson, MO in a grocery store parking lot. We had sung for the owner, Paul, for the last 3 or 4 years. The biggest concern there was getting me on and off the makeshift stage, which was the back of a flatbed truck. I made it fine with the help of the guys. Paul was very pleased with the crowd that gathered to listen and booked us again for next year.

The committee that had booked us for the concert in the city park of Dexter, MO, for the 4th of July had called and cancelled. Their celebration was not going to be held that year after all. That was okay, we would have our own celebration here at our house, complete with a picnic and fire works after dark.

July 17th.

It was my monthly check up with Dr. Trueblood and once again I had come out packing plaster on my right leg, much to my disappointment. The doctor's nurse told me the same thing she had told mom on another visit . . . that I had set records and broken a few with my recovery. I had never thought about breaking or setting any records throughout my recovery. All I had thought about was getting well as quickly as possible, back to normal and the things I loved to do. I knew I had not done anything in my own power.

July 27th.

The 25th it was 6 months since the accident. I have truly come a long way in 6 months. When I was lying in the hospital in St. Joe I did not have a clue I would be back on my feet and walking 6 months down the road.

We celebrated Mark's 19th birthday tonight with cake, ice cream and presents. Only the immediate family was present but Mark declared it his best birthday ever! That is always good to hear and I was certainly glad to be around to help him celebrate.

August 2nd.

I kept hoping for cooler weather. Summer seemed to just go on and on and I was always hot. The heat of summer had never bothered me much, but this year I had been miserably hot all summer. Mother kept telling me I was probably having "hot flashes" but I thought it was probably the six prosthetic socks I was wearing in the prosthetic leg. Normally a person only wears one nylon sheath and one five-ply sock. However, as my leg healed and the swelling continued to go down, it got smaller and the prosthetic leg got bigger. I read one time that the feet are the body's thermostat. Since I had lost a foot and a half I had decided my thermostat had gotten stuck on at least 105 degrees.

When I was walking around the house I had gotten into the habit of not using the walker. I would stay close to the walls and furniture using them for support. It was working just fine for me until I stepped the wrong way on the threshold between the living room and kitchen and lost my balance and fell flat on my bottom just like a toddler. It had jarred the whole house and both Kent and Mark came running to see if I was okay. They found me still sitting on the floor laughing like a hyena. I assured them I was just fine and they helped me up and I went on my way. That was my first fall.

August 18th.

Kent got a call from Gold City the 18th. They were in need of a substitute drummer the 22, 23 & 24th and wanted to know if he would be interested in the job. We only had one concert on the 23rd and we encouraged him to go for it. Playing in the band for one of the top Gospel groups would be a good experience for him and we would find someone to fill in for him. We called Jim Stevenson, Dean and Sandy's son, and asked him if he would sub for Kent. Jim said he would. I got Kent off on Friday morning to meet up with Gold City and that night we rehearsed with Jim. Mark walked him through the songs in rehearsal and he did just fine at the concert, although he said he was a little nervous.

My voice had gained in strength now but I continued to have the hoarseness in a certain area. I did not have as much trouble with it when I sang the tenor part as I did when I sang soprano on a solo. As far as standing and moving around while singing, that was getting better although I was not confident enough to move around very much. And the mic cords were a problem. If one got around one of my feet, I could not feel it and it would trip me up. I was hoping time would help, as well as the prosthetic on the right foot when I finally got the cast off. Perhaps then I would feel more stable and free to move around.

August 27th.

I went to Dr. Trueblood's for the regular check up and cast change today. However, this time I got a shock. When he looked at the x-ray he saw that the tibia had stopped healing. The gap had not completely filled in and it had just shut down. Dr. Trueblood said that it sometimes happened that way and when it did we could take other measures. One option was a bone stimulator to encourage the bone to start healing once again and the other was bone grafting. He wanted to try the stimulator first and had the nurse put one on order. He said I would probably have to wear it for 3 months and after that time if it had not done the job we would try bone grafting. I came from that appointment a bit discouraged and very disappointed. This was the first setback since the reaction to the blood transfusion in St. Joe.

August 28th.

We went to see Gold City and The Hinsons at the DuQuoin State Fair tonight. I think they were all surprised to see us and especially to see me up and walking. Ronny was very inquisitive about my injuries and my prosthesis.

After the concert Gold City followed us home and parked where we used to park our bus out back. We visited a while before everyone turned in. Around 2:00 or 3:00 AM Tim was having a problem with his back. The next morning he asked if we knew of a Chiropractor in our area. We located one for him and Kenny took him there for an adjustment. The rest of the guys straggled in and out throughout the day and kept the shower going as they cleaned up. I kept the coffee pot on and food on the table for them until time for them to leave out for their next concert. It was a fun time for all of us.

September 8th.

I got a call from Dr. Trueblood's office that the bone stimulator was in and for me to come in so it could be installed. The old cast was cut off and a new one put on. Two holes were cut in the cast, one on each side of the fracture site. The electrodes for stimulating the bone would fit in the holes. The wires going from the electrodes had to be attached to the battery pack I wore at my waist. Every day the electrodes, and my skin they were in contact with, had to be cleaned and recoated with KY Jelly. The battery pack also had to have a new battery everyday so the bone would be continually stimulated to grow. There was a beeper that would go off if the stimulator were interrupted for any reason. I could only hope that the stimulator worked because it surely was a nuisance!

The little beeper proved to be a real panic! The first night I wore the thing to bed we had just gone to sleep when it went off and I could not figure out how to shut it off. I finally took the battery out until I could make adjustments then put it back in. Kenny and I both hoped that would not be a nightly occurrence. It was like having the alarm clock attached to my waist. Over the next couple of days I got into a routine of caring for the stimulator and it proved to be easier and less trouble than I had first thought it might be.

September 13th.

Unless I had a doctor's appointment or adjustment at the prosthetic's office things were fairly normal in our household. I was doing most everything except for cleaning. When I cooked, washed dishes and ironed I would sit on the step stool. I could not sit on it for very long at a time or my legs would start hurting. I took it a little at a time, and continued to spend a lot of time on the couch with my legs stretched out to rest them.

We were singing most every weekend, which felt so very good. Our greatest need at this time was the means to buy another bus. Our lawyers were working on a settlement with the milk company but we had been told those things usually take years. That was not very encouraging.

September 27th.

The National Quarter Convention in Nashville, Tennessee would be starting the 29th and go through Oct. 4th. I wanted to go so badly but decided I had better not try it this year. I had always looked forward to going to the convention each year. Kent decided to go for a couple of nights and I would hear all about it from him when he returned. Not as good as going in person but not bad.

Kent left on Oct. 3rd for the last two nights of the convention. After he arrived he called to let us know he would be staying with Gold City. They had rented hotel rooms and had plenty of room for Kent. He was having a good time and said that he had seen Larry Gatlin backstage where the convention was being held. I thought it would have been interesting had he gotten to talk with Larry. Our bus with *Galatians* on the destination sign used to be mistaken for The Gatlin Brothers all the time. Many times there would be a call on the CB radio wanting to know where *The Gatlins* were headed and if they were all on the bus. One time Steve just went along with the guy on the CB and told him, "Yeah, they were all on the bus."

I had been doing well with the stimulator, no more waking up in a panic from the beeper, and I had gotten accustomed to the battery pack at my waist. I was anxious for the next appointment with Dr. Trueblood to find out if it was working. All I could feel was a dull ache in the bone, which had been there almost from the beginning anyway. The next x-ray would tell us what was happening and I was anxious for good news.

October 8th.

Had an appointment with Dr. Trueblood today. The stimulator was working and the bone was once again mending. Hallelujah! I would not mind wearing it for another two months if it continued to work. Bone grafting was not something I wanted to experience.

October 13th.

I got my new left prosthesis today. It is a lot smaller and looks better than the other one. It's a bit more "cosmetic" in appearance although the ankle is still big and ugly. I understood that it had to be that way because my leg is longer than most amputees. Most are just below the knee and those prosthesis have smaller and more natural looking ankles. That was okay; I liked having as much of my leg as I had. It was good for my self-image and I needed that. I could live with a thick ankle on the prosthesis. I was also surprised that the new prosthesis did not have the straps like the first one had. This one had a suction fit. That was very encouraging to me. I would now be able to wear jeans, slacks and closer fitting clothing.

October 16th.

Helen Jo and I had been talking about going to Nashville on a shopping trip for quite a while and finally decided to do it. We had the guys write out directions to Rivergate Mall where we had shopped before. We knew there was a motel near the mall and everything would be right there for us and easily accessible. We made reservations at the motel and finalized our plans. Since Mom was going along too we decided to invite our Aunt Bunny to go along with us. That way Mom would have someone near her age to shop with. Helen Jo would be driving with me as her co-pilot. We planned to leave on Friday morning of the 17th, shop when we got there, spend the night, shop Saturday the 18th and then drive home that evening. We wanted to be back before Sunday the 19th, which was Kent's 24th birthday. We were so excited!

October 20th.

What a good time we had on our weekend trip. It was the first time we had been with Aunt Bunny in a while and we talked and talked. She was interested in my legs and the prosthesis and at bedtime it was, "Show & Tell."

I had done very well walking in the mall. We had paired off. Helen Jo and I had gone together and Mom and Aunt Bunny went together. When I got tired or my legs hurt too much I would sit for a while and tell Helen Jo to go on and shop and I would wait for her. I think I kept up better than they, or I, had expected.

The only problem we had while we were there was when we decided to try to find a pottery and basket place we had seen advertised. We did not know how to get there. We had seen billboards advertising the place and tried to find them again and follow them. Big mistake! Especially in rush hour traffic. What can I say . . . being from a small town we did not know about rush hour traffic! At some point we realized we had made a wrong turn and needed to head back in the other direction. We found a place where we could make a left hand turn and sat and sat and sat waiting for the traffic to thin out so we could get back on the highway. Finally we got a little break, I gave Helen Jo the go-ahead and she floored it, squealing the tires and fishtailing the back-end a bit. And from the back seat we heard Aunt Bunny say, "Weee, Daisy Duke!" We never did find the pottery and basket place but we laughed and laughed about Helen Jo's Daisy Duke.

October 25th.

Gold City stayed with us again between concerts. They were surprised at how well I was doing. We all had a great time visiting and relaxing. Of course, we attended their concerts and enjoyed them. I was glad they were comfortable enough with us to come in and make themselves at home.

November 6th.

I had the usual monthly appointment with my doctor today. Another x-ray and another new cast. The bone was continuing to heal and he said it looked good. Hopefully the cast would be off before Christmas.

We had been practicing a lot on our vocals with Mark coaching us. That little twerp could hear all of the parts and could not understand why we could not hear them. I think he got a little aggravated with us sometimes. He was trying to teach us to hear our parts and stay on them. We tried to explain to him that when you don't hear it, you don't hear it, it was as simple as that. However, we kept trying and doing our best to improve.

We would be singing at a benefit Dean and Sandy Stevenson were having for us November 22nd and I decided to make Helen Jo and I new stage dresses. I did not know if I was up to the job or not but with Mom's help we got them done. It felt good to make a couple of pretty dresses again.

November 22nd.

The new dresses were very pretty although I certainly felt klutzy in mine. With the big old cast and prosthesis with one shoe, there was no way to look dressed up. However, it was good to be walking, standing and performing, well on the road to recovery. Hopefully the clothing and shoe situation would improve with time.

We enjoyed being with the Stevensons as well as all of our friends in the groups that performed and helped with the benefit.

November 23.

The cast had really been bothering me. The whole bottom of the foot part was crumbling away to nothing. I suppose that is testimony to the amount of activity I have been able to engage in. When I was mostly lying around the casts held up much longer. I was thinking I would probably have to go to Dr. Trueblood's the next day and get a new one. I was not going to be able to make this cast last until December 3rd when I had my next appointment.

November 25th.

I had waited as long as I could to have the cast checked. It had continued to deteriorate and I was afraid it would somehow harm my foot walking on the crumbling bottom. I had called Dr. Trueblood's office and explained the situation and was told to come to his office. Dr. Trueblood removed the cast today for good. Hallelujah! I had worn a cast on that leg for eight and a half months. It was a wonderful Thanksgiving present for me.

After my doctor's appointment I was sent to the Prosthetic Lab to be fitted for a temporary filler in my right shoe. I was not sure what to expect as far as the *filler* was concerned. I soon found out that it would not be as shocking and traumatic as my experience with my left prosthesis had been. The filler was made up of half of a prosthetic foot attached to a piece of plastic or fiberglass (not sure what it is made of) which was made to fit the contour of the bottom, sides and heel of my foot. It was slid into the shoe, I put my shoe on and wonder of wonders, I had a whole foot again! I asked the prosthetist about wearing panty hose and he told me that would be perfectly okay. I was glad to hear that. I had worn total support panty hose for years. They made my legs feel better, especially on days when I was on my feet most of the day and half the night. I was anxious to find out if I could get back into them. Since they had always been a bit of a struggle to get on, especially when they were new, I would have to work up my nerve to try them the first time. I was not sure how to go about it, over my "real" legs or over the prosthesis.

When I took my first steps there in the prosthetic fitting room I was surprised at what a difference it made having two feet the same size, and shoes on both feet. It was much easier to walk and to keep my balance. I had been told I would probably start out using two canes to help me walk and would always have to use one cane. I never used two canes. I was using one at the time I got the cast off and used it until after Christmas. I still carry it occasionally to places where I will be in a large crowd because people will give more room to someone with a cane. I walk so well most people would never know I am a double amputee. In fact, I have been chewed out a few times for parking in the handicap parking places, which I have a placard for. If I see someone watching me too closely I just limp a little to put his or her mind at ease.

It had taken all afternoon between the doctor's office and the Prosthetic Lab but I was going home a happy woman, thrilled to finally be cast free, but worn out after the long day.

November 28th.

Thanksgiving! I had so much to be thankful for and I truly was. Our family was all together at Mom and Dad's. For the first time in 10 months I felt almost normal. Just looking at me when I was wearing slacks, most people would never know of my handicap. However, I knew it with every step I took but I believed that would get better with time.

The biggest disappointment after getting the filler in my right shoe was realizing that I would only be able to wear shoes that came to the ankle. Lace up booties or hiking boots would be my shoe wardrobe from now on. I had hoped to be able to wear flat shoes or slippers of some sort. However, with the half foot there was nothing to hold a flat shoe or slipper on, no toes to fill out the shoe to keep it from slipping off. I was very disappointed about it but to wear a different style shoe I would have had to have the half-foot amputated at the ankle too. That was not an option. I would rather be able to walk without canes therefore booties and hiking boots were just fine. Later on I would find that I could also wear low-heeled boots to the knee, which would work with dresses and skirts. However, they did not support my foot as well as the sturdy lace up boots and I did not feel as stable in them. They would only be for wearing on special occasions.

I had gotten up my nerve to try on the total support panty hose when I was getting dressed to go to Mom's on Thanksgiving Day. Although I had not been successful on the first try and had to call for assistance from Kenny to help me get untangled, the second try was successful. It felt mighty good to be all "supported" again. My clothing fit better and they actually helped to give my prosthesis stability. Because of the support they also helped keep the swelling down in the right leg. That leg remained swollen and would swell more during the daytime. The leg is larger than it was before the accident, whether from swelling alone I do not know. There is numbness in many areas, especially where there was a trauma of some sort. It has amazed me that the scar that runs around the calf under the bend of my leg has misplaced nerve endings. I can scratch the scar on the left top near my knee and feel it on the right side of the scar. The scars, which are big and ugly, actually look better with the stockings over them too. Hopefully they would look even better by the time I was once again wearing skirts and dresses. Oh, and with the panty hose, it was *over the prosthesis* on the left and *over the natural foot* on the right.

December 5th.

We rehearsed for a benefit concert for a friend in another local Gospel band who had suffered a terrible head injury on the job and was fighting for his life. He had already survived longer than expected and was improving. His story was much as mine had been almost a year ago. In my mind I was thinking his injury was worse than mine because it involved his head.

December 11th.

It was hectic Christmas shopping and making trips to the Prosthetic Lab for adjustments on one prosthesis or the other and usually both. I got the permanent shoe filler on the 18th. It felt much more stable than the temporary and seemed to hold my foot straighter. Because of the lack of natural toes the foot rolled to the right rather badly. I wanted all of the stability and normal foot action I could get and the permanent filler seemed to provide that. Many people commented on how well I walked.

December 26th.

We had a wonderful Christmas at Daddy and Mom's with plenty of delicious food and lots of wonderful gifts. There's no better way to celebrate the birth of Jesus Christ than with family. At the same time and place the year before, we had never dreamed what lay ahead for us just one month down the road.

December 29th.

Today was Mom's 65th birthday. We went to Dr. Trueblood's office for my appointment and he discharged me from his care. I had walked into his office unaided, not two canes, not even one, much to his surprise. He grinned real big and said something like, "Well, look at you!" His nurses' reaction was about the same as his and they again commented on my recovery. It was good to hear it again, but it had seemed a very long and painful road to recovery to me. We had come to love Dr. Trueblood's nurses, Shirley and Helen, as much as all of the others who had given me such good care during the last eleven months. And we loved and appreciated Dr. Trueblood too. Turned out he was a very good doctor, just as Carolyn had said, and quite personable in a dry sort of way. After heartfelt thank yous and hugs all around we left for home.

December 31st.

When I had been lying in ICU in St. Joe there were many things I wondered about. Many things I had thought I might never be able to do again. Things I loved and enjoyed doing. One of those things was hosting the New Year's Eve party each year in our home. The boys always looked forward to the party from year to year and early on in our singing career had decided they did not want to book anything on New Year's Eve. I never knew how many people they would invite and never cared. The more the merrier. We would play games and eat holiday goodies into the wee hours of the morning, adults, teen-agers and little kids. When someone got tired they would find a couch or bed or spot on the floor to curl up on and sleep. I was very happy to be preparing for that party this year. Mom had come to help me finish cleaning and getting things in order. I was expecting a house full, as usual.

Two guests I was especially looking forward to seeing were Beth Colman, my favorite nurse from St. Francis and Tony Esnwah, my favorite aide. Tony was a black man who was a native of the Virgin Isles. He had a heavy accent and huge smile. Although I had come to care for him as much as I had all of the other caregivers during my eight weeks in the two hospitals, our first meeting had been more than embarrassing for me. I had called for help to get on the bedside commode and in walked Tony. There had been a male aid at Heartland West Hospital but he had never assisted me with anything as personal as using the pot! Having a male aide was just another thing I had to get used to and I did. My family became quite fond of him too, and he soon learned that my two boys were going to tease him about something at every opportunity. Usually his accent or misunderstanding of a bit of slang or word he did not know or understand. We were all thrilled that they had accepted our invitation to come and party with us on New Year's Eve. Other guests for the first time were the Robinson Family.

It was a wonderful party and the perfect ending to what had started out to be a horrific year. It was our prayer that 1987 would be a much better one. Little did we know that the worst was yet to come.

PART FOUR

By the first year anniversary of my life-changing accident I was getting around better all the time and taking care of my own home. Things were finally back to near normal. I continued to have to go for adjustments to the prosthetic lab now and then but no more doctor's appointments or hospitalizations. The 7th surgery was truly the last.

The men in my family had all told me that when I wanted to try driving to just say the word and one of them would ride with me. January 21, 1987 was the day I decided I was ready. I had received notice that I would have to renew my driver's license on or before my birthday on the 17th of February, which prompted me that the time was right. Daddy happened to be the only one around and I called him and told him I was ready to try driving. It was almost exactly a year since I had driven a vehicle. He drove his car to my house, took the seat on the passenger side as I was getting situated in the driver's seat, and away we went. I found that the only adjustment I had to make was to get my right foot farther up on the accelerator and/or brake pedals so I could feel them with the flesh and blood part of my foot. I had no problem whatsoever. When I went to renew my driver license I had to drive for the license inspector and again had no problems. The only restriction on my license was that I could not drive a stick shift . . . that was not a problem. I never did like driving one anyway. The last time I had driven one many years before I had jumped it down the street like a frog and declared at that time I would *never* drive one again! For several months I drove our truck because I felt more secure in it than a car. It was bigger and higher off the road and just felt safer. We did not have a car at the time but Kenny told me when I was ready for one we would go car shopping. It was several months before I was ready for the smaller feel of a car.

We had continued to sing during the first 2 months of the New Year, ever hopeful that before too long we would once again have a bus and be back on the road as before. We could then pick up our dream where we had left off. However, sometime during December and January Helen Jo and Steve were having marital problems which eventually lead to him moving out of their home in February and a divorce in August.

Early in February I had received a call from Judy Rainforth in Nebraska asking if I would come to their church in Hastings, the one where we were scheduled to sing the night of the day of the accident. The weekend they would like to have me was March 7th and 8th. They would pay airfare for Kenny and me if we could come. We talked it over and decided it would be good for me to make that trip. I gave my testimony at a banquet they were having on Saturday evening and then shared with Judy and Gaylen's Sunday school class on Sunday morning. It was a good and positive experience and I did very well on the planes as well as in the airports.

With the separation of Steve and Helen Jo, The Galatians were now short one singer and rhythm guitar player, but we kept on going as a trio. Our first concert without Steve was February the 28th. We were nervous but did not have any trouble and were accepted very well. Naturally people wanted to know where Steve was and that was uncomfortable for Helen Jo but with the help of the boys and Kenny fielding the questions she made it through.

We were booked every weekend and met every obligation through May of 1987 even though Brad Moore left us the middle of that month. The boys contacted a friend, Dennis Patton, who came and played keyboard for us the last two weekends in May. Our last concert, which was the last Sunday in May, Kent was unable to go. He had not been feeling well for a couple of weeks but continued to work the farm and make the concerts on the weekends. That Sunday we had to leave without him. I don't remember much about how we got through it but Mark and Dennis somehow made musical/instrumental adjustments to compensate for our missing drummer and we made it through. I know my mind was not on the singing but back home with Kent. He was pale and had no energy and continued to have a hacking cough. There had to be more wrong than allergies or a sinus infection.

On June the 2nd we finally got Kent to go to the doctor. Unbeknownst to anyone Kent knew he had lumps in the lymph glands in his groin as well as under his arms. The doctor ordered a blood work-up and Kent was diagnosed with acute lymphoid leukemia (ALL) and immediately hospitalized. One of the nurses told us that afternoon as he was being given a blood transfusion that he would not have lasted through that night had he not been hospitalized. Thus began a three-year fight for his life. What the bus wreck had not been able to accomplish, illness had. The Galatians dreams of a full time ministry were now totally shattered. Kent was in a terrible battle and we all wanted to be there for him to support him. It was especially important for Kenny and me to be with him. He chose to stay in the hospital in Cape Girardeau to be close to home. I understood that fully.

In August Helen Jo and Matt were in dire need of a place to live and Kenny and I were trying to figure out a way to help. We thought of building on to our home but were not sure that was the thing to do. One day Kenny mentioned that a big old two-story house was for sale here in Olive Branch. If we liked it he thought it might be perfect for our family plus Helen Jo and Matt. We decided to take a look at it. I loved it at first sight and so did Kent and Mark. We arranged to buy it and rent our home on the lake until we could sell it. We moved in a couple of days before Christmas 1987 and Helen Jo and Matt moved into their small two bedroom apartment upstairs about a week later. They had been staying in our parent's guest room and the new quarters were a great improvement.

After we were all settled into our new home Kent seemed to become a father figure to Matt who was almost five. He followed Kent around and dogged his steps in the house and in the yard. Helen Jo and Matt lived with us for 3 years until she married a wonderful man, Bobby Jones, who literally lived just down the road from us here in town.

Kent's oncologist had only given him a 10% chance of survival when he was diagnosed with leukemia. Not a very good prognosis but we were believing for another miracle. I felt sure that God could and would do for Kent exactly what He had done for me. After all, I was a miracle and Kent would be too. Kent also had a lot of faith and kept claiming his healing and believing God was doing the work no matter how sick he was or how bad things looked. After his first round of chemotherapy and radiation he gained a remission, which lasted almost two years. I felt sure God had again given us a miracle. When Kent lost his remission in December of 1989 he went to St. Louis for experimental treatment, which actually killed him and did not rid him of the leukemia. He died on March 15, 1990 at the age of twenty-seven. It was difficult for me to understand why Kent was not healed when I had been. I was not mad at God or anything like that, I just did not understand. It was even more difficult for Matt to understand. When Mom was trying to explain to him that Jesus had wanted Kent to come and live with him in Heaven Matt told her, "Well, he can just bring him back!" Then he threw himself on Kent's bed and cried like his little heart was broken.

Helen Jo and Bobby had finalized their wedding plans for March 17th. I was supposed to stand up with Helen Jo. When Kent died on the 15th, they were going to postpone their wedding but we told them not to do that because Kent would not have wanted them to postpone. They went ahead as planned and although I attended the wedding; I did not feel that I could stand up with Helen Jo. She had contacted a friend who filled in for me. Kent's funeral was the 18th, the day after their marriage. They delayed their honeymoon one day in order to be at the visitation the night of the 17th and attend the funeral the next day.

We lost three people from our house that weekend. It was now just me, Kenny and Mark. It was not long until Mark was called to play bass for The Imperials Quartet in Nashville. He accepted the offer and in the beginning was driving back and forth for the weekend venues with them. He soon realized he could not continue the 3 1/2 hour commute, especially in the early morning hours when he would be returning home. He talked it over with us and made his decision to move to Nashville in September of 1990. We were now two for the first time since 1962. And we were still grieving over the loss of Kent.

As a Christian I believe I will see Kent again in Heaven and that gives me comfort. Oh, I miss him every day and think of him every day, and for a long time I could hear his voice as he came in the front door saying, "Hey, Mama what's for supper?" I still grieve for him at times and when I drive by his grave at the cemetery I tell him how much I miss him, even though I know he is not there. I know where he is and I picture him riding a golden chariot full out over the hills of glory, just as he did his three wheel ATV, with that wonderful smile on his face, happy and healthy. And that makes me smile with him.

Eventually I feel I got an answer from God as to why Kent was taken so young. I was reading my Bible one night and the first two verses of the 57th chapter of Isaiah seemed to light up for me. It reads, "The good men perish; the godly die before their time and no one seems to care or wonder why. No one seems to realize that God is taking them away from evil days ahead. For the godly who die shall rest in peace." (TLB) Those verses gave me a bit of peace. I thought if there were "evil days" ahead for him and they were worse than what he had already been through, I did not want him to suffer more.

PART FIVE

During the Desert Storm War I had corresponded with 3 soldiers. One of those young men, Michael Glenn, became very special to me. He was near Kent's age and it was therapeutic corresponding with him. When he returned home to Fort Bliss in El Paso, Texas Kenny and I planned a vacation out that way to meet him and his wife, Letty. Since we were going all the way across Texas we naturally planned to see Dr. Lancourt in Dallas. I contacted him and told him of our plans and he and his wife invited us to spend the night in their home. We arrived there and were greeted with open arms. He could not believe how well I was walking, unaided by even one cane. He called his surgical assistant, who sadly was not Dick, to come over to his house and meet us. Upon his assistant's arrival, I was made to walk for him and prove what a wonderful job Dr. Lancourt had done. He had not changed one iota. We were taken out to dinner for wonderful Texas barbecue and treated royally while we were with them. I was so glad to get to see him again. The only thing that could have made it perfect was for Helen Jo to have been along for the reunion.

In the years since the accident I have managed to live quite normally with my handicap. I remember lying in ICU in St. Joseph and thinking of all the activities I would never be able to take part in again. In fact, I have taken part in all but one. Roller-skating! I have not tried it and if I have any sense at all, I never will, even though Geinger mentioned just recently that she thought Jacob might enjoy learning and she thought I should at least try it one more time. I always loved roller-skating but I do think maybe that activity is over for me at this time. Maybe I'll have golden roller skates when I get to heaven.

I have to admit there are some things I miss being able to do. First and foremost is the ease of, and ability to, throw my legs over the side of the bed and stand up and walk when I get up every morning. And I will forever miss wearing pretty high-heeled shoes. I still look at them and admire them and wish I could wear them. At those times I remind myself that it is enough to be able to walk unaided and clunky shoes really aren't that bad. Red high heels in heaven? Maybe. However, I'm certain they will not hold the same appeal there in that wonderful place.

Over the past 20 years I have experienced many unfortunate incidents with my prosthesis. I have chosen not to bore you with *all* of the details, it is enough to say that I have had the leg stuck on and not been able to remove it until Kenny got home to help me. He declares to everyone that I was red in the face and my hair was all fuzzed out when he came in the door, but I have always doubted that. I was simply very frustrated from tugging and prying while sitting on the couch and on the floor, trying to remove the stuck leg. When he arrived he tried not to laugh when he asked what he could do to help. It was fairly easy for him to pull off but he had a different angle on it than I had.

Another time I literally lost my leg in the gym. While working out on one of the machines it came off and went flying across the room in a perfect arch and fell, fully dressed with sock and shoe, in front of a little 5 year old girl who was apparently not disturbed in the least by the flying leg. I could not get off the machine without the leg on and had to ask the woman with the little girl to hand my leg to me. I was almost hysterical with laughter. To the woman's credit, she never cracked a smile and very graciously picked up my leg and handed it to me. Another day I had the opportunity to thank her for her assistance. She said, "To tell you the truth, I wanted to laugh, but knew I could not do that." I told her she should have because it would not have bothered me, after all, I was laughing about it. I asked her if the little girl had said anything on the way home and she told me she had not even though she had expected her to have questions. I guess they see so much in cartoons and such these days nothing much surprises them.

I have fallen a few times because of the unpredictability of an artificial foot. The last time I fell, I used the panic button on my car remote to try to summon my husband to come out and help me up off the porch floor, which I had hit very hard. I found out that day that our car horn will only honk for a certain number of times then it quits. I set it off again! Kenny thought the horn was on television and as it happened he was turning the television off and on at the exact time the horn would start and stop honking. We must have looked like two of the three stooges, both of us pushing buttons and neither of us getting the results we wanted. So much for the benefits of the automobile panic button. Through it all, I have never lost my sense of humor although I might have been perturbed with the circumstances. I would much rather laugh than cry.

At the urging of Phyllis Wilson, our pianist at church, I was finally emotionally able to get back to singing gospel music and hymns. There were many years when I could not listen to gospel music, let alone sing it, and there was still the problem with the hoarseness of my voice. Phyllis kept after me and at one point told me that if I did not use my talent I might lose it. I already knew that but her reminder was a good prompting for me. We started practicing and working on songs, getting the right keys to work around the hoarseness in my throat as much as possible. Then I began singing on Sunday mornings at our church. I found that the more I sang the more strength my voice gained. It was still iffy at times, especially during allergy season, but I was singing again. The songs in the hymnal are almost always high and seldom in the right key for my low voice. However, in spite of that when I was asked to take charge of the music at our church I decided to give it a try. I found that I very much enjoyed singing again, and I have especially enjoyed working with the choir. For Christmas each year we schedule a program of Christmas music the Sunday before Christmas. Those programs have included favorite songs from White Christmas and Jingle Bells to O Holy Night and Away In A Manger. The choir has a good time working on the music and the congregation enjoys the special event. For the 2006 program someone in the choir mentioned the need for a couple of altos for harmony and I agreed. I recruited my sister, Helen Jo, our cousin, Becky Cantrell and a good friend, Mitzi Thomas. After they agreed to help out we set the next rehearsal and upon their arrival lo and behold we had not 3 but 5 added singers. The two bonus singers were Becky's daughter, Lorna Middleton, and Helen Jo's husband, Bobby Jones. Hallelujah, what a choir! On assigning solos and duets, etc. it occurred to me that it would be a good thing for Helen Jo, Becky and me to sing a song together. O Holy Night seemed the right choice and we began practicing. It was the first time the three of us had sung together in 25 years. After a few run-throughs of the song someone commented that we sounded just like the Dixie Chicks to which Becky's husband, Stan, said, "They look more like the Dixie Hens!" Admittedly, we were a little older, but still singing.

Some time ago Gladys Ramage, one of the ladies of our church, asked me if I would record a few songs for her. I told her I would see what I could do then I approached Mark the next time we were in Nashville. I told him of the request and asked if he would accompany me on the keyboard and record it for me. Mark said, "If you're going to do it, why not do it right?" That meant a full band and *serious* recording. That had not even entered my mind and it gave me a lot to think about. I was not keen on recording a solo CD. As I kept rolling the idea around in my mind Helen Jo was always a part of it, I really wanted her to sing with me again. I was a little reluctant to ask her because she is a member of a very large church and was involved in her church's music program. I decided it would not hurt to ask; *maybe* she would like to record again too. I told her about the woman's request and my resulting conversation with Mark, then I asked her if she would like to be a part of it and without hesitating, she said yes. Immediately I thought of Geinger for the alto part and when I asked her she said it sounded like fun. Suddenly we were a trio and it was my favorite kind of singing, three or four-part harmony. We began the process of choosing ten songs and trying to figure out times when we could get to Mark's studio and record. It took much longer than it should have because of work schedules, etc., but the project was recently finished, the CDs have been made and are ready for distribution. We had to come up with a name for our trio and after much discussion and a list of discarded names, "Trilogy," was agreed upon. Even though we could not tour, we could make music and record it. Perhaps the fragments of our shattered dreams were coming together in a new way.

Through the years I have shared my story at every opportunity, both individually and in churches. When I begin I usually ask the people if they have ever seen a miracle before. And then I tell them, "If you have not, now you can say you have, because *I am one.*" I believe that God answered the prayers of His people for me. They were all praying in one accord in my behalf and God heard. I am not special in any way and I am not a miracle because of who I am. I am a miracle because of who *He* is.

ABOUT THE AUTHOR

Deanna Hill is a housewife, mother and grandmother. She resides with Kenny, her husband of 50 years, in the rural community of Olive Branch in southern IL. They live in a big old rambling hunting-lodge-style home on a rather secluded hilltop very near the area where she was born and raised.

She enjoys shopping, reading and painting (with her 90+ year old aunt), but most of all, she enjoys singing. She traveled extensively for 14 years in the 70's and 80's with the family Gospel band. For the past several years she has been music director in the small country church where she has been a member since she was 10 years of age. She especially enjoys leading the church choir in special seasonal musicals . . . recruiting her sister and brother-in-law, as well as several cousins and other singers in the area, to join in the fun.

She spends two days a week with her mother who resides in a nursing home 30 minutes from her home. Every couple of months she is booked in to sing for the residents of the home, which she loves doing.

A couple of years ago Deanna, her sister Helen Jo and daughter-in-law, Geinger completed a Gospel CD as the singing trio TRILOGY. Deanna has been marketing this project very successfully from her home.

As often as possible, though not as often as she would like, she and Ken make a trip to see their son, Mark and his family in Franklin, TN. She delights in and loves being with her two grandsons, Jacob and Ethan.

She does all of this while dealing with being a double amputee, having lost her left foot at the ankle and half of her right foot in a traffic accident in 1986.

Deanna can be contacted through email at deahill@lazernetwireless. net or visit her facebook page at facebook.com and search Red High Heels in Heaven.